# Who the Hell is Plato?

# Who the Hell is Plato?

And what are his theories all about?

## Dr. Karen Parham

BOWDEN
&BRAZIL

First published in Great Britain in 2020 by
Bowden & Brazil Ltd
Felixstowe, Suffolk, UK.

British Library Cataloguing-in-Publication Data
A CIP record for this book is available from The British Library.

Series editor & academic advisor: Dr. Jonathan C.P. Birch, University of Glasgow.

ISBN 978-1-8382286-0-6

To find out more about other books and authors in this series,
visit www.whothehellis.co.uk

# Contents

# Introduction

**Socrates:** *So, Meno, what shall we discuss today?*

**Meno:** *Let's discuss your pupil, Plato.*

**Socrates:** *Yes, Aristocles, or Plato as you like to call him. Very promising pupil. He says he's going to write down some of my conversations.*

**Meno:** *Would they not be his conversations then?*

**Socrates:** *This is true. He may well twist my words. That's poetic licence for you. As long as he uses my method of getting people to think, I don't really mind. I believe he's going to name this method after me – the Socratic Method.*

The dialogue above represents Plato's preferred form of introducing his key philosophical ideas and questions. In most of his works, Plato writes in the form of dialogues between Socrates and well-known public figures of the time: often these are Plato's contemporaries, including his brothers Glaucon and Adeimantus, but sometimes they are historical figures. Socrates, who was Plato's teacher, always features as the one steering the conversations. This scruffy, disrespectful troublemaker (known as the 'gadfly') claimed that philosophy taught him that he knew nothing, and he ridiculed the citizens of Athenian high society, declaring that they too knew nothing. In Plato's works, Socrates and his interlocutors engage in philosophical debates about the nature of reality (metaphysics), what is meant by justice and a virtuous life (ethics), and what is knowledge (epistemology), to name only a few.

Plato (whose name actually means 'broad', possibly referencing his broad forehead, his wide shoulders or his wide-ranging writing styles) is undoubtedly one of the most famous philosophers of all time. Many would agree with the twentieth-century philosopher Alfred North Whitehead's witty remark that the rest of Western philosophy 'consists of footnotes to Plato'. There is hardly a Western philosopher who does not agree with, disagree with, reference or build on the philosophical ideas and discussions of Plato. His use of dialogue and allegories (the most famous being the allegory of the cave) are his signature ways of conveying key ideas, theories and hypotheses. His belief in a perfect world of concepts (his World of Forms) has inspired not only philosophers, but also theologians, religious believers and artists. For them, it is like heaven, the mind of God, or a place of imagination. It is a realm to escape to when things get tough, especially in times of war, famine and conflict. Who would want to stay in an imperfect realm like this, when perfection is possible in the Ideal Realm?

The main aim of this book is to acquaint the reader with many of Plato's works and, in particular, the three key areas of metaphysics, epistemology and ethics that are covered in those works. Those who do know a little of Plato will have come across some of the ideas he expresses in the *Republic*. This is the text that most students of Philosophy are required to read, and some relevant sections will be referred to throughout the book. Although the *Republic* is his most comprehensive work and central to his political philosophy, there is so much more to Plato than questions about justice and the ideal state. There are even more fundamental questions regarding what is real, what we know and what we are, that need to be considered if we are to conduct a thorough philosophical analysis. This is why another aim of this book is to present a holistic picture of Plato's philosophy which, hopefully, will encourage you to read further.

Before looking at Plato's theories, we first need to consider what facts we have about Plato's life. We will then identify those who had the greatest influence on his writings, including his predecessors, his contemporaries and the all-important Socrates. The book will then focus on three key areas and their related concepts: Plato's Theory of Forms, his theory of knowledge and the Good. The Theory of Forms relates to concepts we claim to know. Plato's theory of knowledge is concerned with the concept of knowledge: what it entails, whether we can know, how we can know, and why it is important. The Good is the highest and most perfect of all concepts. This, if any, is the one concept we should try to grasp. While it is exemplified in behaviour, what actually is this behaviour, what does it mean to be good and what exactly constitutes the good life? Plato may not always have the answers, as you will see, but he will show us the way to finding them out for ourselves.

# 1. Plato's Life Story

Plato lived in the fifth century BCE. As far as we know he did not write an autobiography. Indeed, in Ancient Greek society the idea of one would have been ridiculous as the genre didn't exist in the West until the Roman writer, Ovid (43 BCE-17 CE) wrote his autobiographical poem, *Tristia*. Furthermore, for Plato, an autobiography would have been out of character since it is probable he was a modest man given that he chose to make Socrates the 'star' of his dialogues. What we do know of Plato comes from his own dialogues (although some reading between the lines is often needed); from his letters; from his student, Aristotle, and others that took over the Academy; from Diogenes Laertius, the biographer of Ancient Greek philosophers; and from later adherents of Platonism and Neo-Platonism. It goes without saying that a lot of these sources are somewhat

**Fig. 1** Bust of Plato

biased, even fantastical at times, and inaccurate. However, we can still derive a rough idea about Plato's life from them.

## Plato's Ancestry and Childhood

It is believed that Plato was originally named Aristocles, after his grandfather. He was born in 427 or 428 BCE into a respectable Athenian family. If he had not been, he would have received no education and would not have had the leisure time to sit listening to Socrates (c. 470–399 BCE). According to Speusippus (408–339 BCE), Plato's nephew and successor to the Academy, Plato was semi-divine, and his father was Apollo (Greek god of truth and prophecy, among other things). His actual father, Ariston, was a descendent of Codrus, the last king of Athens, while his mother, Perictione, was a descendent of Solon, a famous Athenian lawgiver, politician and philosopher. Plato had two brothers, Glaucon and Adeimantus, and one half-brother, Antiphon, from his mother's second marriage after Ariston died. Like most young men of Athens, Plato was trained in gymnastics, martial arts, music, mathematics, painting and drawing as well as, of course, philosophy. His first philosophy teacher was Cratylus, a follower of Heraclitus, who was a friend of Socrates. It was a rather incestuous and privileged community of philosophers and needless to say there were few if any women. One of the theories that Heraclitus propounded was that this world is in constant flux and that fire was the basic element of the world. Plato would later build on this idea to argue that this world of flux can never be perfect, unlike the Ideal Realm.

At the time of Plato's birth, Athens had been at war for three or four years with Sparta, another powerful city-state in Ancient

Greece. This became known as the Peloponnesian War (431–404 BCE). Plato would probably have had to do military service and he may have even fought in this war as a member of the Athenian cavalry. Sparta eventually won in 404 BCE and pro-Spartan Athenians set up the 'Thirty' as the rulers of Athens. Two of these rulers were Charmides, Plato's uncle, and Critias, his mother's cousin. They were also once pupils and friends of Socrates. Plato dedicates two of his works to these men, his *Critias* and *Charmides*. The 'Thirty' were rich, influential oligarchs whose reign was tyrannical (hence their nickname the 'Thirty Tyrants'); they killed or exiled anyone who opposed them. They even ordered Socrates to bring someone forward for execution, but Socrates refused (*Seventh Letter*). These oligarchs were overthrown in 403 BCE, after ruling for nine months, and democracy was restored to Athens. Socrates' friendship with the 'Thirty Tyrants' may have been the underlying reason for his trial and execution in 399 BCE. It also explains Plato's aversion to democracy. Ironically, in the *Republic*, Plato expounds that democracy leads to the tyranny of the majority, which is perhaps explained by the fact that it was the democratically elected committee of Athens that killed his beloved Socrates. He was probably not the first and would certainly not be the last member of the elite who had an aversion to this form of government.

Plato was an ambitious poet before he met Socrates. He had composed a tragedy, named *The Rival Lovers*, for public performance. Legend has it that after his first encounter with Socrates, he went home and burnt all his poems. We can detect Plato's talent as a poet in his writings and this is why he is appreciated both for his philosophy and his literary skills. It is safe to say that Plato devised a new literary form where poetry (the public performance of lengthy narratives) and philosophy are combined.

## Plato and Socrates

It was at the agora, or marketplace, in 407 BCE where Plato, aged about twenty, first met the 'snub-nosed, goggle-eyed' Socrates (a description given in Plato's *Theaetetus*). From that day on, he became Plato's disciple. An embellished account of their first meeting by Pausanias, a Greek traveller and geographer, reports that Socrates had dreamed of Plato the night before their encounter. He dreamed of a cygnet (swans were birds of Apollo, Plato's supposed divine father) on his lap that instantly grew in size and flew up, making a musical sound. When Socrates saw Plato the next day, he supposedly called out 'That's my bird'.

The two companions were together for at least eight years prior to Socrates being put on trial. If we are to believe Plato's portrayal of Socrates, he was a cunning interrogator keen to pull the rug from under his interlocuters' feet. His irony would often be missed by those quick to attack him, and he would confront those who claimed to have knowledge by demonstrating how little they knew. It was the Oracle of Delphi's revelation, claiming Socrates to be the wisest of men, that spurred Socrates on to find a man wiser

Fig. 2 Bust of Socrates

than him (the Oracle was a priestess who was considered to be the most authoritative and prestigious figure in the classical world). All Socrates knew was that he did not know anything and so the only way of disproving the oracle was to find a knowledgeable man. He quizzed philosophers, politicians and poets but could not find a single wise man. Socrates realized that wisdom was to be found in the acknowledgement of knowing nothing, unlike those who make empty claims to knowledge. Socrates believes the oracle was right: he was the wisest man in knowing this, adding - to avoid being too boastful - that,

> *'the Truth is, O men of Athens, that God only is wise; and in this oracle he means to show that the wisdom of men is little or nothing; he is not speaking of Socrates, he is only using my name as an illustration.'* (the *Apology*)

Inevitably, interrogating everyone he met did not gain him many friends. The *Apology* gives an account of Socrates' defence at his trial against his three accusers – Meletus the poet, Anytus the craftsman and Lycon the rhetorician – who may well have been at the receiving end of Socrates' inquisitions.

Plato was present at Socrates' trial. He heard his teacher defend himself against accusations of atheism and sophistry – two trends in philosophical discourse at the time – and of corrupting the youth. Socrates attempted to demonstrate to the men of Athens that he was none of these. He was certainly not a corrupter of the youth but an educator. In an ironic style adopted from his teacher, Plato portrayed these accusers as the actual corrupters of youth in his dialogues. Tragically, the final verdict was that Socrates was guilty. Socrates could not go against his nature and

**Fig. 3** *The Death of Socrates* painted by Jacques-Louis David in 1787.

refrain from philosophizing and so he accepted that he must die. *Crito* consists of a long discussion between Crito and Socrates on whether he should escape. For Socrates, fleeing would have been tantamount to admitting his guilt and placing himself above the law. Socrates therefore respects the decision of the jury and drinks the poison hemlock. Plato was not there at the end, due to an illness, but there were many who were and who gave a good account of his final discussion on the eternal nature of the soul which can be found in the *Phaedo*. (It was just like Socrates to philosophize, even as he was about to die.) Socrates did not fear death. He believed he would finally be relieved of his corruptible body, allowing his soul to find the true wisdom that he had always been seeking.

## Plato's Travels

After the Athenian state had sentenced Socrates, a good man, to death, Plato believed that this demonstrated only too well that it was unfit to govern. As a result, he left Athens to travel, escaping a democratically run state that he didn't believe in. Plato stopped off in Megara, not too far away from Athens, and lived there for a few years visiting various schools of philosophy. He then travelled on to Italy and there is a strong possibility that he also visited Egypt because of the frequent references to Egyptian practices in his dialogues. If he did visit Egypt, he would probably have met the Libyan mathematician and priest Theodorus who he includes in his dialogue *Theaetetus*.

Plato himself (in the *Seventh Letter*) confirms that he visited Italy and Sicily and became friends with the Greek Dionysius the Elder of Syracuse, described as a tyrant ruler but who had freed the Greeks from possible Carthaginian rule. Carthage was a state in North Africa run by Phoenicians, who ruled and traded all along the North African Mediterranean coast and were eager to add Sicily to their list of conquests. It is believed to be here where Plato became acquainted with Pythagorean theory (see Chapter 2). He returned to Sicily on two more occasions.

## Returning to Athens

Plato returned to Athens in 380 BCE and set up the first ever Academy (our ideas of academies and the word 'academia' are borrowed from Plato). Plato's Academy was built on a plot of land in the north-western part of the city that he bought or may have inherited. It was a sacred olive grove decorated with statues and temples in remembrance of the legendary Akademos, an Athenian hero from Greek mythology whose body is believed to have been buried on the site. At the Academy Plato taught, among other subjects, advanced studies in geometry, the Socratic Method (see

Chapter 2 on what this involves) and his metaphysical theory on reality. The door to the Academy was engraved with the motto 'Let none unversed in geometry come under this roof': a strict door policy, indeed! He would have delivered his theories as lectures but would also have held seminars in order to encourage dialogue in the Socratic way. The Academy did not charge fees for those wanting to learn (or 'recollect', as Plato would have it – see Chapter 4), but his students would have been wealthy enough to spare their time to study there.

Disillusioned by the Athenian leaders and politics, Plato increasingly withdrew into his Academy in order to philosophize with his students. Aristotle of Stagira (384–322 BCE), another renowned Ancient Greek philosopher, attended Plato's Academy for twenty years before going on to teach others, including Alexander the Great. He later founded his own Peripatetic school at the Lyceum. Plato's Academy was not the first of its kind when it was set up – schools of philosophy had been set up ever since the Greeks were first philosophizing. Neither was it the only one in Athens. Plato's rival, the rhetorician Isocrates, had his own school where he taught his students how to speak eloquently and convincingly to an audience. Plato opposed such superficial education and instead promoted the importance of theory and proper reasoning.

The one exception when Plato did involve himself with political life was in 367 BCE, when Dionysius the Elder died and his son inherited the throne. Dion, a friend of Plato's and instructor to both Dionysius the Elder and the Younger, invited Plato to train Dionysius the Younger to be a philosopher king. Unfortunately, the younger Dionysius grew bored of the geometry lessons he had first to master before he could progress to other things, and he rebelled and banished Dion. Plato thought it would be wise to return to Athens before a similar fate or worse happened to him. This was a wise move as Dionysius the Younger soon turned out to be as much of a tyrant as his father. It is likely after these events that Plato wrote his *Theaetetus* and the *Statesman*, less optimistic dialogues on the subject of a philosopher king.

Plato died in c. 346 BCE at the age of 81. Legend has it he died at a wedding party. According to the biographer Diogenes Laertius from the third century CE, Plato was buried in the grounds of the Academy, but there is no archaeological evidence of this. The Academy was passed on to Speusippus, who was in charge for eight years, and then to Xenocrates (c. 396–314 BCE), another of Plato's pupils.

## Plato's Works

Plato wrote extensively and 45 works have been attributed to him, (this includes posthumous attributions and the odd piece written by his students). It is believed that 28 of those 45 works were definitely written by Plato. Thirteen letters written by Plato to friends have also survived. These have been a valuable source in knowing a little more about Plato himself. His works are divided into three periods: the early, the middle and the later works. This is not the most imaginative or informative categorization, and we shall therefore examine each period more closely here in order to clarify how and why Plato's writings have been categorized thus.

## Early Works

The early works are referred to as aporetic, meaning impasse, because these dialogues end without reaching any final answers.

They were probably written after the death of Socrates in 399 BCE but before Plato went on his travels in 387 BCE. Among the most famous of these Socratic dialogues are *Euthyphro*, the *Apology* and *Crito*, which tell the story of Socrates' final weeks before his death and the philosophical discussions he has on issues relating to knowing what justice and piety are, his method of enquiry, why it would be wrong to escape his sentence, and the immortality of the soul. *Phaedo* and *Meno* are two of Plato's later works from the early period, sometimes classified under the middle period. *Phaedo* recounts Socrates' last hours before his death and why he is happy to die. *Meno* investigates what it is to know something and takes the form of a dialogue between Socrates and Meno, a student sophist. Two famous sophists are the subject of *Protagoras* and *Gorgias* from this later early period (Meno was a student of Gorgias). *Gorgias* is often also classified under the middle period because it appears to be an elaboration on Book I from the *Republic*. Finally, other smaller works of relevance from Plato's early period include *Lysis*, a piece on friendship, *Charmides* on self-knowledge, *Euthydemus* on sophistry, *Hippias Major* on praise, *Hippias Minor* on virtues, and *Ion* on poets. *Laches* (on military training) and *Menexenus* (a critique of political rhetoric) also belong to this period but their content is of less importance to the themes of this book.

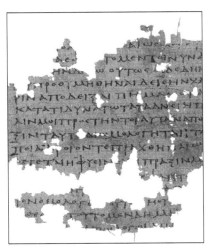

**Fig. 4** Fragment of Plato's *Republic*.

## Middle Works

Plato's next phase of writing contains dialogues that are longer and are grouped together because they have similar metaphysical themes and may have been written in the same period (possibly between 380 and 360 BCE). The most famous of these middle dialogues is the *Republic* which contains Plato's famous allegory of the cave as well as other analogies and allegories (symbolic narratives). These are all meant as illustrations in explaining what is meant by justice, the main theme of this work. The *Symposium* and *Phaedrus* are two works on the nature of love also from this period. *Theaetetus* is another work where Plato endeavours to define knowledge, and highlights the problem of sense perception as a source of knowledge. Sometimes *Cratylus* is categorized under this period. This work discusses whether language is arbitrary or linked to the things they express. Plato's middle period concludes with *Parmenides*, a work that exposes the problems with Plato's theories. The works that follow *Parmenides* are an attempt to rescue his theories in the face of these oppositions.

## Later Works

The final phase contains seven works that were written after *Parmenides*, possibly between 355 and 347 BCE. *Timaeus* is one of these and explains the creation of the world and the preordained order of the universe. This, together with *Critias*, were two parts of a trilogy. The third part, *Hermocrates*, was never written. The *Sophist* and the *Statesman* were two works that were also meant to be part of a trilogy but which were never finalized. The third part being his proposed *Philosopher*, which he never began. The *Sophist* is about the understanding of words and how this should be clear before attempting to define and discuss things. The *Statesman* outlines the next best type of ruler as philosopher kings are no longer a practical option in this imperfect world that relies on the senses rather than true knowledge. *Philebus* discusses the good life, and his last and longest work is the *Laws* which addresses political theory, and psychological, ethical, epistemological and metaphysical questions.

## Plato's Legacy

Plato's legacy to Western philosophy is incalculable and certainly beyond the scope of any single volume, let alone this slender book. We are fortunate enough to have his public writings in their entirety, whereas only fragments of other ancient philosophers' writings have survived. In the case of Aristotle, only lecture and research notes are extant. It took time for some of Plato's works to materialize but when they did, they certainly left a mark in some form or another.

After Plato's death, the Academy went through two periods. The 'Old Academy' continued to operate under the tutelage of Speusippus and Xenocrates after him. They taught the mathematical structures that underpin reality and that reality is built on a single principle of unity. The second period – the 'New Academy' – changed focus. Plato's dialogues often end in an impasse (aporia) and this gained him the reputation of being a sceptic. It is this side of Plato that persisted under the 'New Academy' (until the Academy was destroyed in 86 BCE by the Roman dictator Sulla). Luckily copies of Plato's works, and perhaps the originals, were also kept in the great library at Alexandria before this fell into decline and eventual ruin with sections of it being burned down. Another wave of Platonism was also circulating in this period. This was Middle Platonism, initiated by Antiochus of Ascalon (c. 125–68 BCE) and further defended by Philo of Larissa (c. 159–84 BCE) and Plutarch (45–120 CE). This school rejected the scepticism of Plato and claimed that we can know true and false things about life. The Middle Platonist Alcinous, from the second century BCE, wrote a philosophical textbook based on Platonism, in which he described the Forms as ideas in the mind of the One, or God. This paved the way for the acceptance of Platonism into Christian, Muslim and Jewish doctrines.

Towards the end of antiquity, in the first few centuries CE, Plato's theories were modified by others to form a new philosophy, now known as Neoplatonism. The mystical writings of Plotinus (204–270 CE) belong to this school. Plotinus equated the Form of the Good with the One, the principle of all Being. Porphyry (c. 234–305 CE), Iamblichus (245–325 CE) and Proclus (412–485 CE) developed Neoplatonism further with their own adaptations. There is evidence of Platonism in the works of the early Christian theologian Origen of Alexander (c. 185–253 CE) and Plato's dualisms are also apparent in John's Gospel. Neoplatonism entered Christianity under the Church Father, Augustine of Hippo (354–430 CE). Augustine, in his *City of God*, comments on the ideal state and how Plato came close to it in the *Republic,* but Plato made the mistake of assigning the creation of the world to lesser gods. Still, Augustine appreciates Plato's dualism of this world versus the eternal Ideal Realm, which is easily translatable into Heaven.

*Timaeus* was the only work that was known to the medieval West. The rest of Plato's dialogues were kept alive by Islamic philosophers, enough for them to re-emerge in Western Europe when the Aristotelian-dominated Middle Ages was coming to an end. There were a few scholars sympathetic to Platonism during the Middle Ages, such as Boethius (c. 477–524 CE), but most were unaware of Plato's vast oeuvre. The revival of Platonism was made possible by the discovery of Plato's other works by Cosimo de' Medici (1389–1464) and translated into Latin by the Italian Catholic priest Marsilio Ficino (1433–1499). As well as Ficino, the Italian nobleman Giovanni Pico della Mirandola (1463–1494) and the German philosopher and theologian Nicholas of Cusa (1401–1464) were among those carrying the torch for Platonism in the Renaissance. This form of Platonism is known as Platonic Orientalism as Plato was seen as one of many religious teachers from a line of succession that could be traced back to the earliest sages from the Orient.

One of the major shifts in thought to happen in the West was the discovery of a heliocentric universe (that the earth revolves around the sun and not vice versa). Renaissance men laid the theoretical and methodological groundwork for the establishment of this theory: Nicolaus Copernicus (1473–1543), Galileo Galilei (1564–1642), who believed he had verified this with his telescope (although empirical proof did not come until the eighteenth century), and Johannes Kepler (1571–1630) who introduced elliptical orbits. Galileo agreed with Plato that students should have a good grounding in mathematics. Kepler may have come to his support of Copernican heliocentrism by considering Plato's Sun analogy (see Chapter 5). It was during this period, in 1578, that Henri Estienne (c. 1528–1598), the French classical scholar known as Stephanus, published Plato's dialogues introducing the standard style of citation (based on the division of each page into sections a, b, c, d and e) that is still used today. (The page numbers in our modern printed books don't always match with those larger pages of 1578.)

Interest in Plato faded during the seventeenth and eighteenth centuries due to the rise in empirical science and materialist philosophies of nature among other things, but it didn't disappear altogether. René Descartes (1596–1650), coined as the father of Modern philosophy who laid a foundation for Enlightenment science with his mechanical explanations for physical phenomena, has much to thank Plato for. He, like Plato, was a rationalist, a dualist and a mathematician. He believed that the mind, that is the soul, was a radically different substance from the body and survives death. He also believed that only maths and other *a priori* knowledge provide certainty, not sense experience. The Cambridge Platonists, with members such as Henry More (1614–1687) and Anne Conway (1631–1679), were a group of English scholars from the seventeenth century who revered the works of Plato and Plotinus. Their belief in faith and reason being reconciled was founded on their interest in Plato.

The nineteenth century saw a revival of interest in Plato. Thomas Taylor (1758–1835) renewed interest in Plato with his new translations of his works that added a mystical twist. This appealed to some of the Romantics, including the poet William Wordsworth (1770–1850). More serious study of Plato as a philosopher was conducted by John Stuart Mill (1806–1873) and George Grote (1794–1871), who didn't necessarily agree with his philosophy but did give him credit for his methodology. Benjamin Jowett (1817–1893), whose translations you may read, made Plato publicly accessible. He made the *Republic* a central text to classical studies, which is still the case to this day.

This brings us up to the present day, where Platonism is still apparent in the works of logicians such as Bertrand Russell (1872–1970) from Anglo-American philosophy (Analytic), and Edmund Husserl (1859–1938) from European philosophy (Continental) among others. These are but some of the philosophical traditions that can be directly associated with Plato.

Plato's influence does not stop there. His literary style, the topics he chose, and his method are apparent in some of the most influential philosophers since. Many have adopted the dialogue presentation of philosophical ideas, such as Scottish empiricist David Hume (1711–1776) or the Irish empiricist and idealist George Berkeley (1685–1753). Søren Kierkegaard (1813–1855), who was a great admirer of Socrates, mirrored himself on the Socrates that Plato portrayed in his dialogues. Ideas of feminism first emerge in Plato's *Republic* (see Chapter 5) but also totalitarianism (according to the liberalist Karl Popper (1902–1994). Last but not least, we have Plato to thank for the subject of philosophy as we find it today in the West. He differentiated philosophical thought from rhetoric and poetry and added an ethical dimension to natural philosophy (early science). He may in fact, have been the first to use the word philosophy. So, the high esteem that is given to the study of philosophy is certainly something we should thank Plato for.

Plato's ideas are not only to be found in philosophical works. His allegory of the cave is often interpreted in spiritual traditions as an image of the path towards enlightenment. Leaving the cave has become a symbol of learning the truth in all sorts of other contexts as well, from discovering true reality in the films *The Matrix* (1999) and *The Truman Show* (1998) to realizations about the human condition expressed in Jeremy Griffith's *A Species in Denial* (2003). There are similar cave analogies used in literature, for example H. G. Wells' *The Country of the Blind* (1904) or Jose Saramago's *The Cave* (2002). Another of Plato's myths from the *Republic* is the Myth of Gyges which was the inspiration behind J.R.R. Tolkien's *Lord of the Rings* (1954–5). The myth is the story of Gyges who lived in Lydia, an ancient kingdom in what is now Turkey. Gyges comes across a ring that makes him invisible. He uses this ring to gain power and become the king of Lydia.

This chapter has hopefully provided you with an idea of Plato, and his talkative avatar, Socrates. We have looked at what we know of his life, the importance of his teacher Socrates, the dialogues, and Plato's legacy. To gain a good understanding of Plato further, it is important to consider what drove him to write about certain topics and choose certain characters for his dialogues. This is what we will be examining in the next chapter.

# Plato's Timeline

## Plato (BCE)

**c.428-427** Plato is born

**407** Plato meets Socrates

**399-390** Plato writes his early dialogues: *Euthyphro*, the *Apology, Crito, Lysis, Hippias Minor, Ion, Hippias Major, Laches, Charmides, Euthydemus, Menexenus, Meno, Protagoras, Gorgias* and *Phaedo*.

**398** Plato leaves Athens

**388-367** Plato writes his middle dialogues: the *Symposium*, the *Republic, Phaedrus, Cratylus, Theaetetus* and *Parmenides*.

**380** Plato returns to Athens

**375** Plato sets up Academy

**367** Plato teaches Dionysius the Younger in Sicily

**361-360** Plato goes a third time to Sicily

**360-347** Plato writes his later dialogues: *Philebus, Critias, Timaeus*, the *Sophist*, the *Statesman* and the *Laws*.

**c.346/347** Plato dies aged 81

## World Events (BCE)

**c.800-701** Homer

**c.570-495** Pythagoras

**c.535-474** Heraclitus

**c.515-450** Parmenides

**c.470** Socrates is born

**c.446-386** Aristophanes

**431-404** Peloponnesian war

**404-403** Thirty Tyrants rule

**399** Socrates dies

**395-387** Corinthian war

**387** The 'King's Peace' or 'Peace of Antalcidas' is drawn up

**384-322** Aristotle

**375** Battle of Tegyra: Thebes is victorious against Sparta

**371** Sparta falls

**357-355** Athens is at war against its allies

**346** Thebes gives way to the rising power of Macedon

# 2. Influences on Plato's Thinking

L et's, for a moment, consider Alfred North Whitehead's remark – that the rest of Western philosophy is mere footnotes to Plato (see Whitehead's quote in the introduction). Viewed negatively, his remark could be interpreted as a lamentation. Friedrich Nietzsche certainty thought so. For him, Plato's influence is world-rejecting. Viewed positively, Plato has given the West a philosophical foundation and his ideas echo all subsequent philosophical thought.

Plato, as with any other intellectual, should not be taken in isolation and is a product of his time. He is a synthesis of his predecessors with his own novel ideas thrown into the mix. In this chapter, we look first at his philosophical muse, Socrates, followed by a consideration of his rivals, the natural philosophers and sophists. A further three philosophers stand out as being worthy of recognition in shaping Plato as a keystone to Western philosophy: Pythagoras (c. 570–495 BCE), Parmenides (c. 515 BCE), and Heraclitus (c. 535–475 BCE).

## Socrates

The most significant philosopher in Plato's life was, of course, his teacher Socrates. Although Plato's Socrates would have quibbled and insisted he was only his instructor, not his teacher, who helped him recollect what he already knew in his soul. In Plato's early aporetic works and his works from the middle period of his life, Socrates is his protagonist. In these works, Socrates always triumphs by making his interlocutors appear ignorant, arrogant or immoral. He is Plato's philosophical hero. It is worth bearing in mind that others may be less impressed with Socrates and his role in Athenian society, his conduct during the trial, and his style of philosophizing.

Considering the leading role that Socrates plays in most of Plato's dialogues, we may be tempted to think that Plato's thoughts do not actually feature at all in these works. Plato hides behind his characters so that we, as his readers, are unsure of his actual views. There is a purpose to this. Plato is trying to encourage us to think for ourselves about the issues raised rather than impose his views on us. It is, however, impossible for Plato to distance himself entirely from what he writes. His views are evident in his choice of topics, his explanations given, as well as the odd conclusion he reaches (if any). It is thanks to Aristotle, Plato's pupil, that we know that the Theory of the Forms is Plato's own and not Socrates', for example. We are tempted to think that Plato used Socrates, a reputed man of wisdom, as a mouthpiece for his own thoughts and theories, but Plato's theories merge with those of Socrates because they are a logical progression from what Socrates had taught. It does not end with Plato either; the dialogue must continue (and it has to this day). Plato didn't want to present a doctrine or treatise set in stone, as many of his contemporaries did. This goes against the very nature of philosophy as Plato understood it.

## The Socratic Method

Plato introduced us to Socrates' philosophical method, the Socratic Method – a method of rational and logical discussion which I will refer to as the *dialectic* henceforth -- used by Plato to get you to think about the meaning of words. This method, also known as the *elenchus* method, involves a proposed understanding of a concept being picked apart and revealed to be insufficient. It has become the modus operandi of much of Western philosophy. You start by asking a question about what something means, and upon further analysis it becomes apparent that there are underlying assumptions which need to be queried. This will lead to further questions as the analysis goes deeper and becomes more taxing. In the *Republic*, Socrates explains,

> '*when it [the dialectic] takes things for granted, it doesn't treat them as starting points, but as basic in the strict sense – as platforms and rungs, for example. These serve it until it reaches a point where nothing needs to be taken for granted, and which is the starting-point for everything.*'

What Plato (as Socrates) means is that the dialectic starts with questions about basic concepts that his interlocuters take for granted, such as virtue, justice or knowledge and examines the assumptions that are being made about them.

In *Charmides*, for example, Socrates, Critias and Charmides examine what is meant by self-control. It soon transpires that they don't know what this seemingly straightforward, common-sense concept actually means. It is not quietness, modesty, doing one's own job or even knowing oneself, as was assumed. The dialectic doesn't expect you to arrive at an answer because most things are laden with assumptions. If you are using the dialectic correctly, one question leads to more questions rather than answers. You must be willing to ask further questions and try and answer them as well as you can. At the end of *Charmides*, for example, the discussion has led them to investigating what knowledge of knowledge is. This is far from the initial inquiry into self-control, which they have been unable to define with any certainty. Most of Plato's early dialogues, after using the dialectic, end with aporia (impasse) for a reason. He wants the interlocuters and you, the reader, to use the dialectic and not simply fall back on easy answers.

Not averse to a bit of oratory himself, Plato's Socrates resorts to speeches – involving rhetoric and opinions – in those cases where the interlocutors are unable to ask the right questions or answer them. Their ignorance means they are unable to deal with the dialectic and so they must be told rather than them exploring the issues for themselves. A good example of this is in *Ion* where Socrates has to inform Ion, with two long speeches, because he is unable to use the dialectic and work out for himself why reciting Homer's poetry is not a skill.

## Socrates the Midwife

In *Theaetetus*, Plato describes Socrates as a midwife. Plato's birthing allusion may be a sly reference to the fact that Socrates' mother was a midwife. In a metaphorical sense Socrates acts as a midwife to give birth to philosophical ideas. Ancient Greek midwives were often barren themselves and Socrates is barren of wisdom; he claims he has no knowledge and he is prohibited 'from having any offspring'. Socrates ('with god willing', he adds) is responsible for drawing out the knowledge from the patient. It is there but it needs a professional like Socrates to bring it out of them. Sophists are unlikely to draw this out of their clients. Instead they impregnate them with ideas from the outside world. Socrates has the task of eliciting the processing of those ideas further so that the student realizes their error. Midwives were also match-makers, and Socrates match-makes his students with the right ideas. Theaetetus is pregnant with knowing what knowledge is but needs Socrates to prise it out of him. In this particular dialogue, Theaetetus has given birth to a stillborn; no satisfactory answer to the question of what knowledge is has been found. The dialogue ends with an aporia and both Socrates and Theaetetus agree that they do not know what knowledge is and can, therefore, not know anything. Socrates has been a midwife to many, including Plato himself. Plato's dialogues, including this one, are a demonstration of his own skills as a midwife: he guides the reader through Socrates' process of the dialectic so that we might give birth to our own satisfactory answers.

## Socrates the Gadfly

Plato informs us in the *Apology* that Socrates was aware that he had acquired the moniker 'gadfly' and, indeed, embraced the nickname. The gadfly buzzes around livestock annoying and biting them, just as Socrates annoys his interlocutors by asking them probing questions they often fail to answer. Plato believes this is Socrates' task and that God gave him to the state as a gift: 'the state is like a great and noble steed who is tardy in his motions owing to his very size, and requires to be stirred into life'.

For Plato Socrates is irreplaceable and for this reason his life should be spared. Moreover, he should actually be kept and fed by the state for this service that he provides. Plato makes it quite clear that Socrates is only a gadfly to those he believes are redeemable, others less worthy only get a speech from him. It is indeed a privilege to be bothered by Socrates!

In *Theaetetus,* this student mathematician is portrayed by Plato as showing much potential as a philosopher. He admits to not knowing what knowledge is, which is taken as a good sign. Plato's Socrates can then get to work on him properly and the dialogue can go into philosophical depths. By the end of the dialogue they still don't know what knowledge is, but Theaetetus is content with this. He has realized that all his previous beliefs about knowledge were false and now he has the ability to consider new ones and see if they pass the elenchus test. Plato must have gone through the same rigorous examining by this gadfly and it certainly paid off.

## Know Thyself

While Socrates is on trial, he explains how 'the life which is unexamined is not worth living' (the *Apology*). This can refer to either the external world around us or the internal, contemplative life that reflects on the working of the soul. Socrates, and therefore also Plato, favoured the latter. This is apparent in *Theaetetus,* where Socrates digresses in the middle of the dialogue in order to deliver an encomium (a speech or piece of writing which praises) in recognition of the mental life. Plato, like Socrates, would much rather consider 'what is it to be a human being? What behaviour or experiences are proper to just this being and differentiate it from all others?' and not to notice 'what his neighbour is up to'.

This admission comes after a discussion of Protagoras' reliance on sense perception as a source of knowledge. He is concerned with the active life and how things come and go and not the superior mental life that contemplates the soul and what is eternal. Only the eternal can give us absolute knowledge. This is why 'know thyself' is essential, whereas knowing the world around you is not (see Chapter 4 for more on this aspect of knowledge). Socrates knows himself: he knows his limits and he seems to cherish the fact that he knows nothing. It is ironic that the man who knows nothing but his own limits is the wisest of all. The aporetic endings of Plato's dialogues are proof that he too considers his limits to knowing the answers.

While Socrates is Plato's philosophical hero in his early works, Plato begins to have doubts towards the end of his middle period and the later period where he shows the limitations of Socrates' theories. In *Parmenides*, Socrates struggles to defend his Theory of Forms and is taught a lesson by Parmenides (see Chapter 3 for an explanation of Plato's Theory of Forms). But it is a young Socrates who has not yet learnt the dialectic properly and is not yet exercising the method to his full ability. This doesn't mean that Parmenides wins either. Parmenides can't offer a satisfactory alternative and so Socrates' Theory of Forms ends up being the better of the two theories. In the *Sophist* Socrates features only in the beginning as a young and impressionable man. In the *Statesman* the young and the old Socrates are only used as examples of how the Theory of Forms doesn't work because the young Socrates doesn't have the same properties as the old Socrates and so neither can participate in the Form of Socrates. The main interlocuter in both these dialogues is instead the Eleatic stranger, a representative

**Fig. 5** *The School of Athens* painted by Raphael between 1509–1511. All the philosophers depicted sought knowledge of first causes. Plato and Aristotle appear as the central figures, with Socrates to the left, engaged in a philosophical debate.

of Parmenidean thought from the ancient town of Elea. In Plato's last work, the *Laws*, Plato does the unthinkable: a text without Socrates. Has Socrates gone out of favour or is Plato just more confident in stepping out on his own?

## Physicists and Sophists

The Platonic dialogues highlight the importance of a dialectic, where opposing theories are discussed and lead to new theories and new domains of examination. In this respect, it is important to look at Plato's predecessors and contemporaries, whose weaknesses and flaws he builds on dialectically. In the *Apology*, the Athenian judges accuse Socrates of being an atheist and a corruptor of the youth. In his defence, Socrates refers to two disreputable philosophical schools of thought that he rejects: the natural philosophers, or physicists, and the sophists. Plato seconds this in many of his early works where he demonstrates Socrates' innocence and how his philosophy clashes with that of the physicists and the sophists, who, he says, were actually the ones blaspheming and corrupting the youth.

## The Natural Philosophers or Physicists

The pre-Socratic physicists 'investigate things beneath the earth and in the heavens', from worms to weather events! (the *Apology*). The philosophers Plato is referring to are Thales (c. 624–548 BCE), Anaximander (c. 610–546 BCE), Anaximenes (c. 585–526 BCE) and Democritus (c. 460–370 BCE), a contemporary of Plato. Plato was not interested in these types of questions and considered them a threat to moral and political order. According to the atheist physicists, nature is non-teleological, meaning that everything is understood to be purposeless and atomized. Even morality is scrutinized in this way. As a consequence of this approach, there are believed to be no natural moral laws. Morality is for the individual to decide, against the better judgment of family or the city. While Plato disagreed with the physicists, without these non-mythological accounts of nature, he would not have developed his own teleological explanations for natural phenomena that we read in *Timaeus*, for example. Plato, ever the committed scholar, believes that there are teleological explanations for everything in the world. The reason why we have long intestines, for example, is so we are not constantly eating, and we have time to philosophize (according to the *Timaeus*).

## The Rhetorical Sophists

The sophists are the nephews of the physicists, according to Socrates. If moral laws are arbitrary, as the naturalists claim, then you can manipulate words to get what you desire. This is precisely what the sophists did. Sophists were distinguished foreigners who would travel around teaching citizens how to win any argument, 'to make the weaker argument stronger' even. They had no established schools of their own and instead would pay flying visits to various cities, rather like travelling salesmen, trying to persuade people to pay for their services. The absurdity of sophistry is a re-occurring topic in Plato's works. Many of his dialogues are named after sophists, *Gorgias* and *Protagoras* being two examples. From these two works, we can detect that Plato had a certain admiration for Gorgias (483–375 BCE) but not for Protagoras (c. 490–420 BCE). Gorgias, although he was a sophist, is more genial to Socratic teaching, whereas Protagoras is full of his own self-importance, presenting an encomium (eulogy) in praise of himself. Students of sophists also feature in the dialogues. *Meno*, the title of another one of Plato's earlier works, was a student of Gorgias. He is portrayed as not being as knowledgeable as he first thinks he is. He is unable to explain what virtue is and where it comes from and yet he still claims that he is virtuous. Plato ends this dialogue on an ironic note by submitting to Meno's wisdom in knowing that he is virtuous, despite not knowing what it is.

The sophists' main weakness, and a glaring one, is their inability to engage in the dialectic which would lead them to knowledge. They are only capable of delivering speeches and using rhetoric. According to Socrates (and therefore Plato), this is not genuine teaching as it does not lead to knowledge. Instead, it is a battle of words that leads to blurred meanings and a lack of truth about anything. An example is Protagoras who was famous for claiming that 'man is the measure of all things'. What this amounts to is that there is no one source of truth or value and everything is relative to the knowing subject. Sophists give provisional definitions, using examples that are unlikely to cover everything, rather than offering something universal that will provide a more adequate definition. This is illustrated in *Hippias Major*, for example, where Hippias defines commendation or giving praise by giving examples of what you praise. A 'fine-looking girl', 'an Elean mare', 'a lyre' and 'a pot' can all be praised for their fineness, but this doesn't help us define the act of giving praise. Attending to superficial definitions, as this dialogue demonstrates, leads the sophists only to ambiguity.

Socrates may have seemed like a sophist to outsiders, but any similarity is superficial. Poets, such as Aristophanes (c. 446–386 BCE), are partly to blame for this image. In his plays, Aristophanes made Socrates look like a sophist by portraying him as foolish, impious and a corrupter of youth. He gives the amusing example of Socrates conducting an experiment to see whether a gnat hums through his mouth or through his rectum. While many of his fellow Athenians might have concurred with Aristophanes' parody (seeing the humour in this, not to mention the likeness), Plato makes it quite clear that Socrates is pious and serves the gods, unlike the sophists, who do nothing to improve their fellow human beings. Socrates is concerned with real arguments and knowledge, whereas the sophist is all about appearances and ambiguity. Socrates does not enter into arguments in order to disarm his opponents so he can win. There is usually no satisfying conclusion to his dialogues because Socrates uses argument for the purpose of getting his interlocuters and readers to think, and to provide proof for certain beliefs, not to impress audiences or win an argument. Disarming an opponent is the first stage in getting them to think beyond their established beliefs. Nobody, except Socrates, is a winner in Plato's dialogues because nobody is wise, unless they accept that they know nothing. As we have seen, Plato's most successful interlocutors will be hesitant and aware of their own limitations rather than ready to launch into long speeches about how fantastically learned they are.

## Using Irony on the Sophists

Often Plato's dialogues appear quite comical with their use of irony (meaning 'feigned ignorance' in the original Greek). The sophists are usually at the receiving end of this irony. Socrates exposes their foolish pride and overconfidence for what it is: unfounded. Socrates pampers their egos with tongue-in-cheek compliments. This technique is used to contrast the wisdom of Socrates – his professed ignorance – with the actual ignorance of his interlocutors. Socrates' irony increases with the degree of ignorance of his interlocutor. The purpose of Plato's use of irony is to educate, to provoke the interlocuter and reader into 'knowing thyself'. Socrates' jokes are, therefore, actually very serious.

One of the most ironic of Plato's dialogues is *Euthydemus* from his early period. Euthydemus and his brother Dionysodorus were warriors and are now sophists. Socrates is impressed with their claims to teach virtue and invites them to demonstrate their skills on two of his youthful companions, Cleinias and Ctesippus. They oblige and trick Cleinias and Ctesippus into admitting absurdities through the use of *eristic*. Eristic involves catching people out in logical contradictions by playing with the ambiguous meaning of words. Ctesippus has a dog that is a father and from this the sophists argue that his dog is his father:

*'[Dionysodorus] —You say that you have a dog.*

*—Yes, a villain of a one, said Ctesippus.*

*—And he has puppies?*

*—Yes, and they are very like himself.*

*—And the dog is the father of them?*

*—Yes, he said, I certainly saw him and the mother of the puppies come together.*

*—And is he not yours?*

*—To be sure he is.*

*—Then he is a father, and he is yours; ergo, he is your father, and the puppies are your brothers.'*

They also claim to know everything because they know something, but fail to demonstrate they know something when Socrates asks them to say how many teeth each other have. 'Will you not take our word that we know all things?' they ask. Socrates ends the dialogue by suggesting that the brothers keep their 'skill' to themselves, as it is so valuable and can easily be picked up by anyone in an unpaying audience. Although there is humour here, there is also seriousness. Sophists had the power to corrupt society. They would teach would-be politicians how to win arguments by playing with words instead of using the dialectic and reason. The future of Athens is at risk under this sophistry. Furthermore, claiming to teach virtue, as these two sophists do, is a serious claim indeed and by joking around, they are devaluing the importance of virtue.

As mentioned earlier, Plato is not entirely dismissive of all sophists. Gorgias is respected because his sophistry has some reasoning to it, although faulty. In a piece entitled *On Non-Existence*, Gorgias argues that nothing exists, which lands him in a position where he is unable to know anything; because how can you know anything if nothing actually exists? It is this piece that Plato is referring to in his dialogue *Gorgias*. Gorgias explains that his role as a rhetorician is to persuade. He persuades a doctor's patients to have surgery, for example. In this way, he has a crucial role. He persuades the ignorant by giving them speeches rather than reasoning with them through dialectical discussions. The result is 'that an ignorant person is more convincing than the expert before an equally ignorant audience'.

There is hope for the humble Gorgias yet if he can admit to the superior method of the dialectic. He does so towards the end of *Gorgias*, where he proves useful in his art of persuasion by convincing Callicles to engage in the dialectic with Socrates. Here he acts as the assistant to the soul doctor, Socrates. He has realized that his art of rhetoric is inferior to the dialectic, which has actually taught him what he really is: a philosopher's aide.

## Pythagoras, Heraclitus and Parmenides

Plato and Socrates were great admirers of Pythagorean thought. This is the same Pythagoras we know from school: a mystical mathematician who believed in the immortality of the soul, reincarnation, and that mathematical things were eternal. These ideas are also apparent in Plato's dialogues. He too believes in the eternal soul and reincarnation (as he explains in *Phaedo* and *Meno*, for example). The slave boy in *Meno* is shown to know

Pythagoras' theorem without having been taught it, suggesting that geometry is innate and acquired from the eternal realm of the Forms (see Chapter 4 on the importance of mathematics and geometry). In *Timaeus*, Plato explains how the world and its soul were constructed by the demiurge (creator of the world) according to mathematical principles, something else that is reminiscent of Pythagorean philosophy. Many of Socrates' followers were Pythagoreans. Phaedo, Simmias and Cebes, from the *Phaedo*, were Pythagoreans who were present during the final hours of Socrates' life. They are, therefore, ideal companions to discuss proof for the existence of an immortal soul before the untimely release of Socrates' own soul from his body under the orders of the Athenian state. They are happy to accept that the soul does reincarnate into various bodies but not that it goes on forever. Socrates has no solid proof that it does, but he presents three arguments to show that it might. Together, these three arguments show how the soul is the principle that brings about life, it cannot do the opposite, and so in bringing about immortality, it must also be immortal itself. Socrates proposes that as his is a good soul, it will be able to continue dialectical discussions with the souls of better men when his body dies.

Heraclitus was a pre-Socratic Greek philosopher famous for being obscure. Very few fragments of Heraclitus' works remain. He died a few decades before Plato was born in around 480 BCE, but his influence can be seen in some of Plato's ideas. Aristotle also confirms that his teacher was influenced by Heraclitus, citing Plato's Theory of Forms as an example. Heraclitus made the observation that nothing is permanent in this world, except change. In *Timaeus*, among other dialogues, Plato also describes the world in this way, 'subject to the flow of growth and decay'. It explains further why the world cannot be a secure source of knowledge.

Plato doesn't, however, agree with the Heraclitan idea that there is only one reality, that this world is a reality of flux in which there are no clear divisions between one thing and the next. If this was the only reality, then we wouldn't be able to have knowledge that is certain because everything is constantly changing. Plato considers other realms that might provide knowledge. He is not a complete sceptic and wants to believe there is some knowledge that we can be certain of. He turns to the Ideal Realm, the World of Forms for this (see Chapter 3). Plato alters the Parmenidean idea that the world of sense perception isn't real, to the view that the world of sense perception is less real because it can't be known. For Parmenides it isn't real because only the static can be real. The only thing that is static is the totality of reality, which is one thing and not many things. His view that only one thing exists is known as monism and soon collapses into nothing that can be articulated because words differentiate rather than unify. For Plato words mean something; they derive their meaning from the Forms.

Often the theories in the Platonic dialogues are really a synthesis of Parmenides and Heraclitus. Plato disagrees with Parmenides's monism: belief in the existence of just one thing will mean that you can't speak or know about anything, as that would involve separation from the One. He does, however, like Parmenides' observation that this world we perceive through our senses is unreliable. Heraclitus is right that this world is in constant flux and is made up of many things (it is pluralistic), but he is wrong in his belief that this is the only world that exists. Plato, therefore, combines Parmenides' scepticism of the world of sense experience with Heraclitus' pluralism to develop his own dualism. Plato's dualism consists of two worlds: the imperfect world of flux and the Ideal Realm of perfection.

As this chapter shows, while Plato is undoubtedly an immense figure in the philosophical pantheon, he is still a protégé of Socrates and a product of his time. Without the philosophies of his predecessors and contemporaries, Plato's ideas wouldn't have emerged in the way that they did. This doesn't take away the uniqueness of his work, it simply helps to make sense of what Plato was trying to convey and why he was conveying it in the way that he did.

# 3. Theory of Forms

etaphysics is a branch of philosophy that looks at what exists and what constitutes reality, with special emphasis on those things beyond ordinary sense experience. It deals with the concept of being, existence and the central question of the status of universals (recurring qualities that are exemplified in many things and are themselves unchangeable). This often takes us into the domain of religion nowadays. Most religious people like to believe that there is a reality beyond the one we are currently experiencing. It brings comfort to know that life could continue after death and that that life will be blissful compared to the pain and suffering that exists in this life. Plato was a great believer in a superior realm beyond this physical realm of existence we currently occupy. In fact, he was quite certain of its existence. The main reason for his conviction was not necessarily the comfort of wanting continued existence (although this may have been another reason) but the possibility of there being absolute and unchanging knowledge. As we have seen, this world can't provide knowledge. If there was no possibility of knowledge elsewhere, then we wouldn't know anything with any certainty – something quite unpalatable for Plato, if not for Socrates. Most people believe we can know things and so Plato sought to refine this conviction by identifying what it is we can know for certain. The best candidate, he thought, would be knowledge that stretches beyond this realm of existence and into the eternal. This would be knowledge that is always with us, from birth to death and beyond. For this to make sense, Plato also believed in an immaterial soul. Eternal knowledge resides in our eternal soul.

This chapter outlines what it is that Plato believes exists beyond this physical world. It begins with Plato's Theory of Forms and the differences between this realm of existence and the Ideal Realm. Also included here is Plato's allegory of the cave which he added to help clarify his Theory of Forms. We will also consider Plato's belief in an immaterial, eternal soul that links to his Theory of Forms. Plato has particular ideas about what happens to the soul when it leaves the physical body. This is not quite what you would expect from a philosopher who is ruled by his intellect. Perhaps his renunciation of poetry was not absolute.

## The Ideal Realm, Forms and Particulars

The centrepiece of Plato's philosophy is undoubtedly his Theory of Forms. This theory is first set out in *Phaedo*, from his early period, and is dealt with extensively in the *Republic*. It is also referenced or inferred in most of his other texts. Plato's *Parmenides*, from towards the end of the middle period, marks a turning point in the dialogues as this is where the theory comes under scrutiny and its weaknesses are exposed. From this point on, Plato is more cautious with his theory but never actually abandons it.

Plato developed his Theory of Forms in response to both the natural philosophers and Parmenides. The natural philosophers rely on the empirical and the impermanence of this world whereas Parmenides relies on the logical and dismisses the empirical world altogether. Plato does not dismiss the empirical world and acknowledges the role that this impermanent world has in the development of our soul, but he also accepts that it cannot provide us with certainty or true knowledge. To gain true knowledge, he sides with Parmenides and agrees that logic is a more likely route.

Plato introduces the World of Forms as the origin of true knowledge. This Ideal Realm is a world that is eternal and perfect, an intelligible rather than sensible realm that is 'the source and provider of truth and knowledge', explains Socrates in the *Republic*. The logical argumentation of the dialectic is the only way of catching glimpses of what is true while we reside in this sensible world of imperfection. Things in this world of flux (particulars) 'participate in' (are images or likenesses of) the Forms. Forms help us recognize things in this world: a teapot or a triangle, for example. Forms, and the Ideal Realm where they originate from, offer us some consolation that we can have knowledge and that there is a better, more real world beyond this one.

Recalling, again, the poet Plato once was, the *Phaedo* presents the lyrical idea of immortal souls encountering Forms prior to birth. After being exposed to the Forms in the Ideal Realm – the World of Forms – the soul buries this knowledge when it becomes incarnated into an imperfect, changeable body. This is Socrates' proof that the soul is immortal, and that Forms must exist. In discussion with Socrates in the *Phaedo*, Simmias, convinced by this, states that: 'there is nothing which to my mind is so evident as that beauty, good, and other notions of which you were just now speaking, have a most real and absolute existence.'

Socrates gives another example. Equality is not derived from seeing or hearing or by using any of the other senses and yet we know when things are equal. We must have been born with the Form of Equal (Forms and examples of Forms are usually written with a capital to distinguish them from the ordinary version in this world). The immortal soul must know this Form. It is an audacious leap from eternal notions (Forms) to immortal souls existing.

In *Meno*, Socrates suggests that the soul, after many reincarnations, knows everything from this world and the World of Forms and 'so we need not be surprised if it can recall the knowledge of virtue or anything else which, as we see, it once possessed'. There is nothing that the soul doesn't know (see Chapter 4 for more on the recollection of knowledge). There's hope for us all! It is our soul that recognizes copies of the Forms in this world.

Plato never uses the word Form; this term is something that philosophers have adopted since to explain how these notions or ideas are both something universal – a species – and a shape or mould for something. Forms are archetypes, blueprints, of which we only perceive particular and imperfect manifestations here in our everyday world of impermanence and changeability. Forms, being eternal, existed before the particulars and are perfect in the sense of being ideal and complete. They can be characterized as being unique and as being a pure exemplar of a certain property. Forms are present in particulars and are realized in a multitude of objects and ways. In the *Republic*, Socrates gives Beauty as an example of a Form which is displayed in 'beautiful sounds and colours and shapes, and works of art which consist of these elements'. These things are not identical to Beauty itself; they participate in the Form of Beauty. When we struggle to define our concepts (such as the earlier-mentioned act of giving praise), it may be because of our impartial knowledge of the Forms. Forms are contents of thought and external to the thinker; they are objective and are superior to sense perception. To be able to perceive the Forms enables a person to have true knowledge of things. It reveals the truth of those things, their unchangeable properties. But 'people with the ability to approach beauty itself and see beauty as it actually is are bound to be few and far between', Socrates warns. Does Socrates (or, indeed, Plato) dare to imply he is one of the few? We shall never know!

Particulars are contingent on other things; they are conditional and don't invoke thought. In the *Republic*, Plato (as Socrates) gives the example of the sight of a finger that doesn't impel anyone's mind 'to think and try to come up with an answer to the question what a finger is, since sight has given the mind no grounds for supposing that the finger is at the same time the opposite of a finger.'

When seeing a finger, you don't contemplate whether it is a finger or the opposite of a finger. Particulars don't 'provoke or arouse thought'. The size of a finger, however, does provoke thought. You think about whether a finger is big or small in relation to other fingers. The intellect, not the senses, tells you about size: '[…] the intellect is forced in its turn to look at big and small as distinct entities, not mixed together, which is the opposite of what sight does.' Thinking about these relative properties is to think about examples of Forms (Big or Small in this case).

Particulars are always changing, from being big or small in the case of a finger. It is impossible to 'know' particulars with their non-essential, changeable properties. Luckily there is a reality where things can be known, according to Plato. Forms are those things that can be known because they will be pure, unchangeable and stable exemplars. They can be known but only if you are willing to go beyond this world and into the realm of the intelligent. The more ideal a particular, the more real and good it is, but it can never be as real and good as the Form itself.

It is evident from reading the middle-period dialogue, *Parmenides*, that Plato started to question the viability of his Theory of Forms. Parmenides and his student Zeno are shown to be believers in logical rather than empirical truths. Their position that reality is one and that change is impossible is logical because 'if being is many, it must be both like and unlike, and this is impossible'. This makes them eligible and, indeed, keen to engage in the dialectic with a young Socrates.

> *'Parmenides and Zeno were not altogether pleased at the successive steps of the argument; but still they gave the closest attention, and often looked at one another and smiled as if in admiration of him.'*

Socrates introduces Forms as a possible solution to the problem of things being 'both like and unlike'; a particular can participate in the Form of Like and Unlike. Parmenides and Zeno use the dialectic to criticize the existence of Forms and expose it for its logical inconsistency. The wise Parmenides asks Socrates to consider things that might not have a Form, 'such things as hair, mud, dirt or anything else which is vile and paltry'. Socrates, being young here, is still prone to error and is encouraged, dialectically, to think of all possible scenarios for his Forms. Parmenides asks what should be included as a Form, for example: 'And would you make an idea of man apart from us and from all other human creatures, or of fire and water?' Socrates answers: 'I am often undecided, Parmenides, as to whether I ought to include them or not.' Neither is Socrates sure whether vile things have Forms. For his theory to be consistent, they would have to, but he doesn't like this idea. Parmenides recommends that he continues with the dialectic to find his way out of this predicament and leaves it at that.

Another question to arise in this dialogue is whether a Form participates fully in particulars or just partially. For example, does something small possess Small in its entirety? Parmenides suggests that if it does, then Small can't be present in any other particular. Then again, if it doesn't possess the Form in its entirety, then it can't be unified as it is spread over many particulars. Furthermore, there are likely to be just as many Forms as there are chairs and tables or anything else in this world. Yet another problem is whether Forms participate in themselves. Is the Form Large, for example, a large thing? If Large is large itself, where did it derive its largeness from? There would have to be some other Form for Large to gain its largeness from. Where did this Form get its properties from? This leads to an infinite regress of Forms relying on other Forms for their properties. This famous argument against the plausibility of Forms is known as the third-man argument, making its first appearance in *Parmenides* but later taken up by Aristotle with a vengeance. It refers to the need to introduce a third Form (such as the Form of the Form of

Man) to explain the origin of the Form of Man (and then a Form of the Form of the Form of Man, and so on).

Plato recognizes that belief in the Forms is exactly that, a belief, and he is left with question marks concerning this theory. This has further implications for what we can know and what is good (see Chapters 4 and 5 on these questions). Without the Forms in a superior reality, there is no Ideal Realm to offer certainty and nothing can be known.

## The Allegory of the Cave

Most of Plato's dialogues contain a myth. While we associate myths with Ancient Greece, we don't usually associate them with philosophical writings. Plato must have been aware of the fantastical nature of myths and how they contrast with the reasoned philosophical dialectic in his dialogues. It was, however, customary in Ancient Greek society for myths to be narrated to the public – either by the poets themselves or by rhapsodes (professional performers of epic poetry), actors or dancers – and Plato has to comply with this tradition in order to be taken seriously. Some of the myths Plato uses would have been known by most Greeks at the time through poets such as Homer and Hesiod. Plato often adapts these for the purpose of making a particular point. For example, the myth of the androgyne in the *Symposium* is used to illustrate the shortcomings of Aristophanes. Putting forward a rather moving myth, Aristophanes explains how humans were originally androgynous and, after being split by Zeus, are constantly in search of their other half. Readers are meant to interpret this to mean that Aristophanes is not a complete soul and doesn't understand himself. Often, myths are used as illustrations for those who are not philosophically curious. The allegory of the cave, for example, is an easy way to explain the notion of Forms. More importantly, myths are used to instruct readers about issues that cannot be accessed through our limited minds; for example, in *Timaeus*, Plato describes how the universe came to be. A mechanistic explanation, like that given by the natural philosophers, is insufficient, not to say impossible. A more comprehensive account requires teleology or purposes, reasons why the universe is here, and myths provide this. Myths can mirror truths whereas literal language – a product of this impermanent world and the imperfect bodies living in it – can't even come close to the truth.

For someone who ostensibly rejected poetry, Plato returns to literary creativity quite often. As well as using the traditional myths, he invents his own. The allegory of the cave is probably his most famous and is used to illustrate the plight of the philosopher in finding true knowledge, knowledge of Forms and the Form of the Good.

'Imagine people living in a cavernous cell down under the ground,' Plato begins. These people have lived there 'since childhood, with their legs and necks tied up in a way which keeps them in one place and allows them to look only straight ahead'. All they can see are shadows cast on the wall in front of them. They think that these shadows are real because it is all they can know. This represents the view of most people: that shadows and images of things are real. At a considerable distance behind these prisoners is a fire burning. There are people in front of the fire carrying artefacts as they walk along a road. It is these people who are responsible for the shadows. One of the prisoners is set

**Fig. 6** An illustration of The Allegory of the Cave from Plato's *Republic*.

free and sees the fire. The fire hurts his eyes at first but then he sees and realizes that the things that he could see when he was chained down were just shadows cast by the artefacts. He has reluctantly discovered that the shadows are not real, that 'what he's been seeing all this time has no substance, and that he's now closer to reality and is seeing more accurately, because of the greater reality of the things in front of his eyes.'

These 'things in front of his eyes' represent objects detected through the senses. The prisoner will realize that they too are an illusion once he goes outside into the world. He escapes the cave by 'being dragged forcibly away from there up the rough, steep slope […] without being released until he's been pulled out into the sunlight'. This represents the dialectic liberating our ability to perceive truth. In escaping the cave, he has entered true reality, the World of Forms, which he doesn't yet appreciate. It is only once his eyes have become accustomed to the sunlight that he will be able to see 'real' things. He is able to see the planets in the night sky at first. These signify the Forms. While it is almost impossible for him to see the sun itself, he would work out that it is the cause of the seasons and for everything that exists. The sun represents the highest Form, the Form of the Good, that is the source of all other Forms. The Good illuminates the World of Forms: 'it is responsible for everything that is right and fine [...] and in the intelligible realm it is the source and provider of truth and knowledge.'

Analogous to the prisoner learning the truth about the cave, the philosopher discovers the truth about the Forms. The prisoner is eager to inform the other prisoners in the cave about what he has found and returns to them. Back in the cave, he can't see very well as he has been blinded by the sun. He tries to tell the others about what the shadows really are, but they are not interested and think he has ruined his eyes and is insane. The prisoners are more interested in discussing the shadows than being freed. Just like the sophists, they don't want to learn the dialectic. They are happy with speeches and illusions instead and certainly don't want to listen to the philosopher who is describing another world. The sophists would prefer to stay in the cave (representing ignorance) and encourage their clients (the prisoners in the cave) to believe their sophistry (shadows in the cave) is true.

## The Body and the Soul

Both Socrates and Plato are dualists in two respects. They believe there are two worlds: this world of sense experience and the World of Forms. By extension, they also believe that humans are made up of two things: the body and the soul. The mortal body is a product of this world of flux whereas the eternal soul is of the Ideal Realm. The soul can take us beyond the limits of this realm of space and time and into the realm of thought and ideas.

The soul is one unified thing responsible for animating the body. At the same time, it is also divisible into three parts that are the sources of our motivation. Plato explains his tripartite view of the soul in the *Republic*: there are the rational, the emotional and the appetitive parts (see Chapter 5 for how these parts relate to being virtuous). When a soul inhabits a body, it becomes divided as our motivations conflict with one another, but the true nature of the soul is to be impervious to the body. In *Phaedrus*, Plato compares the divided and disharmonious soul to a winged chariot driven by a black and a white horse. Before the soul is incarnated into a body, she 'traverses the whole heaven in divers forms appearing; - when perfect and fully winged she soars upward.'

Once in a body, the soul's wings lose their feathers and settle on the solid ground. It becomes susceptible to temptations in the physical plane of existence which are evil, and this causes the soul to lose its divinity. In order to redeem itself, the soul must use reason to gain control over bodily temptations (appetites and glory), analogous to the charioteer gaining control of the chariot. The charioteer sitting in the chariot needs to control both horses. The chariot represents the reasoning part of the soul that reigns in the white horse (the spirited part of the soul that loves glory) and the black horse (the appetitive part of the soul). If the charioteer manages to keep the horses under control, then the chariot will 'upward glide in obedience to the rein'. In other words, if we can apply self-control by using our rational part, our soul can grow its wings back and glimpse heaven again. If we let our soul be driven by physical desires, then it is tantamount to letting the horses control the chariot. Our soul is no longer virtuous, which is comparable to the horses' wings becoming damaged and the chariot falling back into this world of change and matter. Whenever we fall in love, Socrates explains to Phaedrus, we see an image of perfect beauty in that person we have fallen in love with. This causes our soul's wings to grow again. But the horses still need to be kept under control. Should we ever be persuaded by another to surrender to our sexual desires and let the black horses reign, be warned that this 'will send you bowling round the earth during a period of nine thousand years, and leave you a fool in the world below.' It is better to pursue true love that involves wanting to perfect another's soul as this will result in being reincarnated into a philosopher's body, which will bring us closer to heaven again.

Plato is also a radical dualist in believing that the soul lives on after the death of the body. This is described in the *Phaedo*, when Socrates explains where his soul is likely to go once he has drunk the poison hemlock. True philosophers prepare themselves in life for this parting of the soul. They learn to distance themselves from physical pleasures which they believe only cause confusion and lead to mistakes. Philosophy is 'the practice of death' by freeing the soul from the errors of the body, and Socrates' soul has 'had the desire of death all his life long' so it can be rid of 'this mass of evil'.

The *Phaedo* describes the next step after souls leave the body. They are judged by their allotted spirit, which determines their fate in the afterlife. Ordinary souls are carried to Hades where they are taken on a tour. The 'wise and orderly soul is conscious of her situation' and listens to the guides and quickly finds her way out, whereas those who have 'long been fluttering about the lifeless frame and the world of sight' will spend more time going through 'many struggles and many sufferings' in Hades. Evil souls who have committed crimes will have no guides at all. The philosopher's soul who has rejected physical pleasures and focused on learning will have gods as guides. They will not need to return to a body but can continue to a heavenly place where they can resume their philosophical discussions with like-minded others. This will soon be Socrates' fate as he is just about to drink the hemlock.

This topic was clearly a preoccupation for Plato as the theme appears again in *Gorgias*, where he says more on the judgement of the soul. The good orderly soul is taken to the 'isles of the blessed', whereas the morally corrupted soul goes to Tartarus where he undergoes the appropriate treatment. At first – 'in the time of Cronos' – people were 'tried during their life-time by living judges on the very day on which they were fated to die'. This led to a perversion of justice. The nobility, who could afford expensive adornments, were able to fool the judges into thinking they had good souls by their appearance. To prevent this error of judgement, Zeus decided to judge people after the death of their body so that it was their true self on trial. This true self contains all the features the soul was born with together with the behaviour they have displayed throughout their life. Virtuous behaviour will be rewarded after death. 'That is why', explains Socrates, 'dismissing from consideration the honours which stimulate most men's ambition, I shall keep my gaze fixed on the truth and aspire to perfection.'

Towards the end of the *Republic*, we learn all about the actual judgement procedure of the soul from Plato's telling of the Myth of Er. A man named Er, son of Armenios of Pamphylia, was killed in battle but came back to life. He was able to tell everyone what he had experienced as his soul journeyed with other souls through Hades. The first place he arrived at judged those souls that were moral. They were decorated with 'tokens to wear on their fronts to show what behaviour they'd been assessed for'. They went through an opening on the right, up through the sky, and were told 'to listen and observe everything that happened in that place'. The immoral souls went through an opening on the left and downwards and had to wear tokens that showed their past deeds. There were two further openings. Wretched souls from below appeared out of one. They had been floating around down below for a considerable time and had received a penalty that was tenfold for every crime they had committed. Blessed souls from out of the sky appeared out of the other opening. The same principle applied to the amount of rewards they received for their good deeds. Souls gathered to tell others of their experiences. After this, they journeyed on to a place where they were given a lottery ticket. When their ticket was called, they chose the circumstances of their next life. Those who had been through the sky tended to choose the life of a tyrant, being unaware of the punishment that would lie ahead of them in the underworld. Before being reborn, all souls were appointed a guardian and drank water of forgetfulness. They fell asleep and were awoken by thunder and an earthquake and then 'All of a sudden, they were lifted up from where they were, and they darted like shooting stars away in various directions for rebirth.'

The idea of reincarnation is usually associated with Eastern religions. In Plato's day, the Vedic tradition (the source of modern-day Hinduism) held such beliefs. Plato may have become acquainted with Vedic beliefs via the Pythagoreans or during his travels to Sicily and beyond. What is more probable is that he was acquainted with the Orphic tradition, quite unlike the Vedic tradition and popular among most Athenians of Plato's time. Orphism was the worship of Dionysus and Persephone who both ventured into the underworld. When people die, their souls are believed to be held in the earth by Persephone until she releases them to be reborn. The Orphic tradition, in worshipping Dionysus the god of wine and chaos, encouraged drinking to induce frenzied states that were meant to purify the soul.

Plato's variant of Orphism involves purification of the rational soul by moving out of the cave of sense experience and towards the Forms. The means of attaining Platonic ecstasy was through the dialectic, not through wine, whereby the soul achieves a vision of the Forms. It becomes more virtuous and, therefore, purified, in recollecting knowledge from the World of Forms. Plato believed Socrates would be released from the cycle of birth, death and rebirth because his soul was pure and wise and therefore able to realize the true reality of the World of Forms.

# 4. Theory of Knowledge

Epistemology, the study of knowledge, is foundational to philosophy and is one of the first modules taught in academic Philosophy. All institutes of learning, whether this is primary school or university, claim to teach knowledge and we all assume we know things. Plato shows us how we should question those assumptions, especially if we don't even know what knowledge is. He helps us understand that we first need to discover what it is we can know, where knowledge comes from, what knowledge is and what branches of knowledge there are before we can proceed with certainty about anything we claim to know. As well as Plato's answers to all these questions, this chapter also addresses Plato's reasons for why knowledge is so important, why love of knowledge is the highest kind of love and why self-knowledge should be a person's first priority.

## What We Can Know

The answer to what it is we can know was covered in the previous chapter when we looked at Plato's Theory of Forms. We can't know anything in this world of flux because it never remains the same. But we can know the eternal Forms. As a consequence, Plato has given us a clue about what knowledge is. It is something objective, true and forever certain. This is what distinguishes it from subjective opinion. Why is this not knowledge? Plato would say that subjective opinion differs from person to person and is not something that can be taught. To teach something, it must be constant and something that can be passed on to others without it changing. Plato considers anything experienced through the senses to be subjective opinion. In *Theaetetus* he explains:

> *'...knowledge is not located in immediate experience, but in reasoning about it, since the latter, apparently, but not the former, makes it possible to grasp being and truth.'*

This rules out any of what we now call the Sciences as sources of knowledge because they are based on observations – in the natural world or laboratories – using the senses. The Sciences, like the natural philosophy of Plato's time, only deal with opinion. According to Plato, the Sciences should focus on the unchanging, certain and true Forms because they provide us with the essential nature of particulars in this world, not observations. Teachers of knowledge should be employing the dialectical method – not what would become the scientific method – as this facilitates our recollection of knowledge that lies within our souls. We need to reconnect with what we were born with (innate knowledge) and not think we can learn anything new from this world. This world only reminds us of what we already know from the World of Forms.

## The Simile of the Divided Line

In the *Republic*, Plato presents the simile of the divided line to illustrate the difference between opinion (what we experience in this world) and knowledge (of maths and the Forms). Plato proposes that there are four things which we claim to base our knowledge on: images and objects from the visible realm, and maths and the Forms from the intelligible realm. He places these four things on 'a line cut into two unequal sections', which should be viewed in ascending order. The two lowest sections only give us opinions, not knowledge, but they are the longest pieces on the line because most people rely on them.

The lowest section represents a state of mind fed by 'shadows, reflections (on the surface of water or on anything else which is inherently compact, smooth and bright), and so on'. This is when information is gained about an object, such as a tree, from gazing at its shadow. This way of acquiring knowledge is inadequate, Plato says, because it doesn't provide any details of the colour, shape or size of the tree. We just know it is there. The next section represents the beliefs we form based on our sense experience. But this, too, does not provide us with knowledge about the object, as the senses deceive and we are only perceiving a particular, not the Form itself.

Through effort and mental discipline, it is possible to advance up the line, into the intelligible realm, and attain knowledge. Mathematical reasoning allows us to progress to the third section of the line. Here the interest is not

> 'in visible forms as such, but in the things of which the visible forms are likenesses: that is, their discussions are concerned with what it is to be a square, and with what it is to be a diagonal (and so on), rather than with the diagonal (and so on) which occurs in their diagrams.'

Maths doesn't deserve the highest position because it still requires images – the use of diagrams and symbols – and 'takes for granted things like numerical oddness and evenness, the geometrical figures, the three kinds of angle' which it doesn't investigate further. Maths mediates between opinion and pure reason by positing hypotheses and subsequent conclusions based on observations. Contemplating the Forms, on the other hand, is true knowledge relying solely on pure reason. True knowledge is achieved by searching for first principles underlying hypotheses. These first principles may destroy the original hypotheses but can also lead to new hypotheses in a process of dialectic. These first principles are the Forms.

## How Can We Know?

In *Phaedo*, Plato (as Socrates) explains how the soul must have existed before it was incarnated into a body because of the knowledge we have of things before we have experienced them. For example, the soul perceives particulars in this world and notices the defects. The fact that it recognizes the defects is proof that the soul must know the perfect version, the Form. Here the soul is recollecting, 'recovering that which has been forgotten through time and inattention'. But how does this recollecting happen?

In *Meno*, Plato explains how recollecting knowledge of geometry works by practising it on one of Meno's slave boys. The slave boy appears to have no prior knowledge of geometry (geometry being something we can know, like the Forms). Socrates asks him questions, where the slave boy only needs to answer 'yes' or 'no'. In this way, Socrates is applying the dialectic by eliciting answers rather than teaching the slave boy geometry.

The slave boy is able to demonstrate that he does know geometry, hasn't been taught it and so must have had this knowledge all the time. Plato's point is that we never learn new things, we only recollect things we already know. Recollection is done through the dialectic; it reveals what our soul already knows.

What Plato is suggesting here is that if the slave boy (or anyone else) already knows the answer to question y, it is pointless for them to search for the answer, since they already have the answer. But if they do not already know the answer to question y, it seems that it is also pointless for them to search for the answer, since they would not know what they were looking for and so could never know when they had found it. If we are to avoid the latter, there must be some sense in which we already know the answer to the questions we ask, hence Plato's theory of recollection.

## What is Knowledge?

Plato is the originator of the tripartite theory of knowledge, a theory defining knowledge in terms of its three components. It was the accepted definition of knowledge up until the twentieth century. In *Meno* and *Theaetetus*, Plato looks at what conditions are necessary for there to be knowledge.

We have already seen that knowledge has to involve certainty, and so it follows that it must be unfailingly true. Truth is, therefore, one of the conditions for knowledge. Truth must apply to a belief, this being the second element of knowledge. Beliefs are what are thought to be the case. In some cases, true beliefs count as knowledge. In *Meno*, Plato asks Meno whether he thinks someone who knows their way to Larissa is as good as someone who has true belief about the right way to Larissa. In this case, it doesn't make any difference. The man who has a true belief will lead you to Larissa because his belief is true. But there is still a difference between someone having a true belief (or right opinion) and someone knowing.

As Plato explains: '...the man with knowledge will always be successful, and the man with right opinion only sometimes.' The man who *knows* his way to Larissa has certainty and is always right. This is why knowledge is more important and why it involves more than having true beliefs. Plato explains to Meno how true beliefs are like untethered magical statues made by Daedalus (a craftsman in Greek mythology). If they are tethered, they are more valuable as they are unlikely to disappear. True beliefs must be 'tied down' to the truth, otherwise they are likely to be forgotten. He continues:

> *'True opinions are a fine thing and do all sorts of good so long as they stay in place; but they will not stay long. They run away from a man's mind, so they are not worth much until you tether them by working out the reason.'*

The third element needed to tie true beliefs to knowledge is a rational account, which we now understand as justification. Plato suggests this in *Theaetetus*, although it is never confirmed as the dialogue ends in the usual aporia. In this dialogue, Socrates explains how he dreamt that in order to analyze something, you need to find out its constituent parts that cannot be broken down any further. Knowledge's constituent parts are beliefs that are true and that can be accounted for rationally (justification for the true beliefs). Philosophers like to present this formally in the following way:

S (the subject) can know P (the proposition or
factual statement that is claimed to be known) if
(and only if)
P is true
S believes P
S is justified in believing P

So, Socrates (subject) knows that 'the man he is talking to
is Theaetetus' (proposition) because it is true (it is Theaetetus).
Socrates believes that 'the man he is talking to is Theaetetus'
and Socrates has justification for believing that 'the man he
is talking to is Theaetetus' (Theaetetus was introduced to
Socrates by Theodorus and Theaetetus did not deny he was
Theaetetus). The conditions of justification, belief and truth are
independently necessary and jointly sufficient for there to be
knowledge that 'the man Socrates is talking to is Theaetetus'.
You'll be glad to hear that that's the last we will be hearing of
Theaetetus. Well almost.

## The Importance of Knowledge

Plato's ethics provide us with a further understanding of the
importance of knowledge (see also Chapter 5). To be good and
act ethically is to be virtuous but to act virtuously, we need to
know what virtue is. For example, we need knowledge of what
justice is so we can act justly. Exact definitions are essential to
knowing things; they give us knowledge of those things. The
opposite is ignorance, which is evil as it leads to corruption,
according to Plato. In the case of Meno or Protagoras (in the
texts named after them), Plato demonstrates how they do not
know what virtue is and so they are miseducating their students

and the public at large. Informing the Athenians that virtue is pleasure, as Protagoras does, has led to Athens becoming unjust. Unjust cities are likely to be full of crime and corruption (putting to death wise men like Socrates, for example) and lose in battle (as Athens did in the Peloponnesian War).

For Plato, the ultimate purpose of engaging in the dialectic and acquiring knowledge is to discover truths about how to live a moral life. By participating in the dialectic, you become virtuous by realizing the limits of your knowledge about this world and yourself. Realizing these limits is invaluable knowledge because it means you won't mislead yourself and others into thinking this world has certainties. This is good and moral behaviour. Acquiring pure, true and precise knowledge is what a good life is all about. It is not about pleasure, as Plato thought most people think. Plato explains in *Philebus*, how knowledge causes the good in the good life and pleasure does not. Knowledge has more affinity with truth, moderation and beauty. Knowledge requires reason and reason is truthful, moderate and beautiful. If you thought otherwise, Plato puts you straight: 'Well really, Socrates', says Protarchus, 'No one, asleep or awake, has ever seen or suspected the slightest trace of any incipient or existing or possible blemish in reason and intellect.'

A good life should, therefore, involve reasoning and knowledge (as the outcome of that reasoning). As we are all born with the capacity to reason and gain knowledge, according to Plato, then we are all able to live a good life. We are all able to maximize our potential for gaining knowledge by using our reason and it is important that we do so.

# Mathematics and Geometry

As we have already seen, Plato was a great admirer of mathematics and geometry. The inscription alone, on the entrance to his Academy – 'Let none unversed in geometry come under this roof' – tells us this. As Plato explains in the *Republic*, part of his ideal system of education requires the younger citizens to be instructed in mathematics for at least ten years (see Chapter 5). Mathematics and geometry, in being concerned with logic and the establishing of universal axioms and coordinates, are secure and are therefore one of the candidates for knowledge. They are of a similar nature to Forms in being concerned with unchangeable universals that we experience examples of in this world. For instance, twoness can be recognized in two cows or two gloves. Plato believes that mathematics is a prerequisite to understanding the Forms. By understanding maths, you are exposed to universals and so you are prepared to 'see' the Forms in your mind's eye.

*Theaetetus* is a dialogue between Socrates and two mathematicians, Theodorus and his student Theaetetus. Theaetetus confesses to having thought about defining knowledge before but admits, 'anything I come up with is unsatisfactory [...] and yet, for all that, the question hasn't stopped niggling me.' This is exactly what Socrates wants to hear: 'this isn't lack of fertility, Theaetetus. You're pregnant, and these are your labour pains.' Socrates is just the midwife to help with those labour pains. Unfortunately, the labour pains deliver nothing as they reach an impasse in defining knowledge (see also Chapter 2). However, as Socrates is conversing with more able interlocutors – mathematicians – the dialogue is able to reach new heights in recognizing the value of an impasse. Furthermore, it goes beyond discussing the physical and focuses on matters concerning the mental and contemplative life. Those dialogues that feature sophists don't venture into these domains. Such interlocuters are incompetent in Plato's eyes, and only concerned with the art of persuasion.

In *Timaeus*, Plato applies his interest in mathematics to the composition of the universe. Essentially, he sees the universe as being made up of triangles – the simplest geometric shape. The elements that make up everything on Earth (earth, air, fire and water) comprise triangles that form four of the five Platonic solids (an Egyptian invention, not Plato's). The Platonic solids are the five three-dimensional shapes that meet the criteria of being regular, congruent and polygonal. Earth is a cube, air is an octahedron, fire is a tetrahedron and water is an icosahedron. The final solid is the dodecahedron, which is the shape of the universe itself. Arbitrary perhaps, but Plato believed that the whole reason for why the universe is there at all, is so that we can learn maths.

Not content with just the universe, Plato dissects epistemology mathematically in *Philebus*. He makes the distinction between practical and educational branches of knowledge, where educational knowledge is purer because it involves thought. In order for any practical skill to count as knowledge, it must involve maths. Music has very little to do with maths, Plato says, and is more about guesswork (ironic considering great musicians of the Western tradition, such as Bach, have had a high regard for mathematical precision and geometric simplicity). Socrates explains:

*'consider the playing of stringed instruments, which uses guesswork to pinpoint the correct length of each string as it moves. Consequently, there is little in it that is reliable, much that is uncertain.'*

Building, on the other hand, is a more precise practical branch of knowledge; it requires maths and precision in measuring things and 'they use ruler, lathe, callipers, chalk-line and an ingenious try-square'. Ancient Athenian builders obviously had a better reputation than our own!

Plato further divides maths into applied and philosophical maths. Warfare and farming relate to applied maths: 'they add two armies together, or two cows'. Measurements in geometry are abstract and count as philosophical maths. The highest branch of knowledge is, of course, the dialectic, which is 'the truest' science of all. Although maths provides the same kind of certainty, it is the dialectic that is superior because of the way it thinks and the objects it deals with. The dialectic uses the intellect and reason in search of truth and is the purest of knowledge.

## Love and Knowledge

Plato discusses physical and non-physical love in three of his works: *Lysis*, *Phaedrus* and the *Symposium*. *Lysis* is a short piece that contrasts non-physical love in the form of friendship (*philia*) with physical love in the form of sexual desire (*eros*). Pederasty, where boys and men had intimate relationships, was socially accepted behaviour in Ancient Greece (with the passive partner being younger and of lower rank). Less so, it would seem, for Plato. In *Lysis*, a youth in his mid-teens named Hippothales has sexual desires for Lysis, who is only slightly younger than him.

Hippothales asks Socrates for advice on how to gain Lysis's interest. Lysis is friends with Menexenus of the same age. They feel philia towards one another as opposed to eros. Socrates demonstrates the superior nature of their friendship as opposed to the sexual desire that Hippothales feels for Lysis. Philia is reciprocal, whereas eros is one-sided. Philia wants what is best for the other: their happiness and the freedom to do what they want in cases where they know what they are doing. Socrates gives the example of driving a chariot (another chariot!). If you don't know how to drive a chariot, then you shouldn't be given the freedom to drive it. If you don't have knowledge of something but think you do, a true friend will prevent you from making a fool of yourself by stopping you in your tracks. This is what Socrates does, although whether he is a friend he cannot say because by the end of the dialogue:

> *'we've now made utter fools of ourselves, [...] since these people will go away and say that we're friends of one another [...] though we were not as yet able to find out precisely what a friend is.'*

Most of the interlocuters in Plato's dialogues teach but don't actually know what it is they are teaching. As a true friend, Socrates helps them attain some knowledge. He introduces them (and his readers) to the highest kind of philia: philosophy or the love of knowledge. This can help you find the highest kind of knowledge: knowledge of the Good. Once you have this knowledge, you can only do good things, according to Socrates.

The first kind of 'love' to be considered in the *Phaedrus* is a purely selfish and appetitive love. It is a corrupting kind of desire that leads to both parties being harmed through the one person wanting to possess the other. Socrates considers this to be the opposite of love. Love should be concerned with the good of the one who is loved. We fall in love because we see an image of beauty in the other person.

Socrates goes on to explain how this kind of selfless love is a good kind of madness. It is a blessing from the gods that helps us perfect our immortal soul. To fall in love with someone is to recognize the Form of Beauty in them and then draw this Form out of them; perfect them by improving their knowledge of this Form (perhaps not quite how we might see loving someone today). In so doing, we perfect ourselves and become more attractive and valuable to the other. Socrates is doing precisely this to Phaedrus by instructing him about love; Phaedrus becomes more knowledgeable and his soul becomes more organized and perfect in the process. In this way, both Socrates' and Phaedrus' souls are one step closer to the divine. Socrates (and Plato) loves all those he instructs in this way. He teaches them philosophy which is about perfecting their souls by helping them find out what they know. This is true love that is interested in souls, knowledge and truth and not bodies, opinions and gratification. Socrates confirms:

> 'But nobler far is serious pursuit of the dialectician, who finds a congenial soul, and then with knowledge engrafts and sows words which are able to help themselves and him who planted them, and are not unfruitful, but have in them seeds which may bear fruit in other natures, nurtured in other ways – making the seed everlasting and the possessors happy to the utmost extent of human happiness.'

In the *Symposium,* Plato (as Socrates) discusses other misunderstandings of love before presenting the right one. First is the kind of love that sophists, who have an underdeveloped soul, believe in. Most of them think love is all about having unrestrained sexual desires. Aristophanes (a poet Plato loathed because of his wrongful portrayal of Socrates as foolish) claims love is about finding our other half. He presents the myth of the androgyne as an illustration (mentioned in Chapter 3). According to this myth, humans were originally androgynes. They were:

> 'round and had four hands and four feet, back and
> sides forming a circle, one head with two faces, looking
> opposite ways, set on a round neck and precisely alike;
> also four ears, two privy members, and the remainder
> to correspond.'

These androgynes tried to climb Mount Olympus and enter the realm of the gods. As a punishment, Zeus split them all in half. Ever since, humans have been longing for their other half. They are incomplete and only another can complete them.

At the other extreme of misunderstanding love, is Agathon who is in love with himself. He doesn't need anyone else to love and considers everyone else to be dull compared to him. This kind of narcissism isn't love because Agathon can't love himself when he doesn't even know himself. He can't see that he lacks knowledge, wisdom and depth.

Socrates comes to the rescue and gives his account of what love is, which he was told by a woman named Diotima. A rare appearance by a woman! She explained that love is a longing in the soul for the Forms. She gave Socrates the example of *'beauty only, absolute, separate, simple, and everlasting, which without diminution and without increase, or any change, is imparted to the ever-growing and perishing beauties of all other things.'*

When we fall in love, we see an image of the Forms of Wisdom, Truth and Beauty in others. We progress from loving others' bodies to loving one body and then to loving their soul. From loving the soul, we learn to love the Forms and eternal realities. This longing for eternity is what drives us to perfect our soul and the soul of our beloved. Love is a drive towards the perfection of the soul. Therefore, as unlikely as it sounds, 'the gadfly' may well be the best lover to have.

All three of these works on love point to non-physical love of knowledge as the highest and best kind of love. This is what Platonic love and a Platonic relationship means. It is a love of wanting to know and wanting to help the other know. This attainment of knowledge is what makes a person wise. A philosopher, being literally a lover (from *philia*) of wisdom (from *sophia*), values the love of knowledge above all else. This is why love of knowledge is the starting point for philosophy.

## Self-Knowledge

The first invaluable step to knowing anything is to 'know thyself'. This is the underlying message throughout Plato's dialogues. We must know our limitations with respect to what we can know in comparison to the gods. The gods have knowledge and are immortal. We lack knowledge and are mortal. We need to practise virtues of temperance, self-control and self-knowledge by letting the rational part of our soul dictate.

In *Charmides*, Plato makes it apparent that Charmides (who turned out to be one of the Thirty Tyrants and unable to contain his earthly desires) is already a lost cause, despite being under the tutelage of Socrates when he was young. He doesn't know himself and so can't have any self-control. Charmides admits as much at the end of the dialogue when he says, 'But heavens, Socrates, I don't know whether I possess it or whether I don't.' Socrates, on the other hand, knows himself and his limitations. He has self-control. Even when drinking wine, in the *Symposium*, we see that Socrates does not let the wine go to his head and cause him to lose control: 'and the most wonderful thing of all was that no human being had ever seen Socrates drunk.' Socrates is divine-like. He reveals his bare, purified, immortal soul stripped of any earthly attachments. This is a necessary requirement for engaging in the dialectic for the sake of finding true knowledge and recognizing the Forms.

Plato presents knowledge as something we should cherish and love. This justified true belief is difficult to find but worth the struggle when we do. If we know ourselves, our limitations, this is half the battle as we are then able to identify what it is we can know. We can know perfect, eternal Forms and Socrates has demonstrated – in the Meno's slave-boy argument, for example – how our souls can recollect this knowledge through the use of the dialectic.

# 5. The Good

Most of Plato's dialogues are concerned with how to behave and what is considered good. This is the domain of ethics. For Plato this is more important than natural philosophy – knowing what the universe is made up of – or rhetoric and winning arguments. Now that we have established what Plato thinks exists (his metaphysics) and what it is we can know (his epistemology), we will look at what he thinks is meant by the Good and how to live a good life. This is expressed in his virtue ethics, which examines where virtues could come from, whether they can be taught, who is likely to be virtuous and qualify to govern others, what the source of all virtues is, and how a person can lead a good life worthy of the gods.

## The Origin of Virtue

A distinction is made in the *Laws* between virtues (divine goods) and health, strength, wealth and beauty (human goods). Virtues contribute to human flourishing and are the determining factor in deciding what we do with these human goods. Virtues are, therefore, the *only* good and a good life is reliant on virtues to dictate our behaviour in every corner of life. If we are to live a virtuous life, how do we acquire these virtues?

Plato doesn't think they can be taught. Protagoras, in the dialogue named after him, defends the position that they can and uses a myth to back his claim. Prometheus (the Titan god of intelligence) gave humans the gifts of fire and technical skills which he had stolen from the other gods. However, this was not enough for them to defend themselves. An additional gift was needed, and so Zeus instructed Hermes (the messenger god) to teach all of humankind justice and conscience. These two virtues provided the foundation for a civilized society which allowed humans to thrive. Protagoras believes that this is still the case and these virtues are not innate but taught. Socrates, by demonstrating how virtue is impossible to teach – because there is no technical skill involved and virtues aren't available to all – is able to enlighten his interlocuter. Protagoras,

> '*who at the beginning supposed it to be teachable, now on the contrary seems to be bent on showing that it is almost anything rather than knowledge; and this would make it least likely to be teachable.*'

Having been reluctantly won over, Protagoras ends his conversation with Socrates in an aporia.

So how are virtues acquired? Virtues are not passed down from the virtuous, we learn in *Meno*. If that was the case, then the sons and pupils of Pericles (a successful and virtuous leader) would have been virtuous, but they were not. Meno, a sophist, believes virtues can't be taught and this is consistent with the sophist's idea that teaching is about rhetoric and not knowledge. If it is not something that can be known, then it is not something that can be taught. Socrates proposes they are recollected by engaging in the dialectic. This technique enables us to discover the essence of a virtue and then we can know what a virtuous act might look like. They conclude by agreeing that virtue is given to certain individuals by the gods, to

> *'the oracular priests and the prophets, [...] and to poets of every description. Statesmen too, when by their speeches they get great things done yet know nothing of what they are saying, are to be considered as acting no less under divine influence, inspired and possessed by the divinity.'*

This, of course, is not a satisfactory conclusion for Socrates because it still doesn't answer the question of what a virtue is and 'we shall not understand the truth of the matter until, before asking how men get virtue, we try to discover what virtue is in and by itself.'

## Poets as Teachers of the Good

Ancient Greeks were taught how to behave from the poets (usually Homer, Hesiod or Aeschylus) or from the rhapsodes, who would recite the works of the poets. The Greeks would admire the courage of Achilles or the cleverness of Odysseus and come to recognize these characters as good because of these isolated acts of heroism.

In the *Republic* Socrates considers this a poetry of appearances that appeals to the emotional part of the soul, and calls it 'poetry of pleasure' as it evokes emotions that lead people to do sinful things. Plato recognized that such heroes had their faults and that the poets and rhapsodes, in praising the poets, were teachers of immorality. Odysseus may be clever, but he is also disrespectful to the gods (he curses the gods after the Trojan War) and Achilles kills, pillages and rapes. These are hardly people who should be idolized, even by Ancient Greek standards.

Plato believed that the poets themselves were representers and

> *'A representer knows nothing of value about the things he represents; representation is a kind of game, and shouldn't be taken seriously; and those who compose tragedies in iambic and epic verse are, without exception, outstanding examples of representers.'* (the *Republic*)

In his ideal state, this kind of poetry would be censored. Only good, morally uplifting poetry that educates people about knowledge and wisdom would be allowed. Such poetry is just and virtuous. Plato believed that only hymns to the gods and praises of good men count as good poetry. Plato's own works that praise Socrates are examples of the latter. This is the kind of poetry that would be allowed in the ideal state of the *Republic* and imitates 'the most beautiful and best life' described in the *Laws*. Any other poetry is likely to corrupt.

Good poetry must also have a proper purpose, other than to entertain. Socrates' dialectic is the kind of poetry that has a proper purpose: it is meaningful, it is orderly, and it educates. Plato's dialogues are proper poetry with a proper hero of virtue, knowledge and wisdom: Socrates. He reveals his virtuous soul by telling the truth using the dialectic.

The Platonic dialogues, like the Homeric epics, have a journey motif as well. Socrates takes his interlocuters on a spiritual odyssey towards perfecting their souls. In the *Republic*, the journey starts in the mundane world. This is apparent in the very first words 'Yesterday I went down', indicating that the dialogue starts in this inferior world of change where the masses reside (in the cave from Chapter 3) and then progresses upwards as the interlocuters are educated about the Forms. The journey continues with the dialectic being introduced. Sometimes it is interrupted by sophistry and speeches, which brings the dialogue back down to earth. Sophists are like the corrupt poets; they too entertain rather than educate, and fool ignorant people into believing they are virtuous. If the interlocuters are true heroes, they will allow themselves to be taken back up into the Ideal Realm by engaging in the dialectic.

There is both comedy and tragedy in Plato's works. His are virtuous comedies, using irony that appeals to the mind rather than the slapstick humour used by Aristophanes, for example. Such farcical humour appeals to the masses who are ruled by the emotional part of their soul (an inferior part of the soul as we shall see in the next section). Plato's comedy rescues the soul from the tragedy of such entrapments. Plato's jokes are ultimately very serious in making fun of those things that are truly ridiculous: ignorance, foolishness and vice. His works ridicule sophistry and superficial poetry, while at the same time salvaging potentially good souls. Plato shows how a philosopher, as a teacher of the dialectic, can be a true, virtuous and just poet.

## Justice, the Just City and the Just Soul

One of the most important virtues that Plato addresses in the *Republic* is justice. Plato's understanding of this virtue is much broader than how we understand it today. We might consider it as fairness or righteousness but it also has a darker side: revenge. For Plato justice is synonymous with doing what is right and is a general idea of goodness. It is foundational to understanding ethical conduct. Ultimately, the just person would have knowledge of the Good.

In tackling the question of what is meant by justice, Plato examines, in the *Republic*, how it becomes manifest in the city and the soul. After arguing with the sophist, Thrasymachus, Socrates rules out that justice is about being the strongest and most powerful. Neither is it to gain from immoral acts as criminals do. Justice is, in and of itself, good. The dialectic provides us with an understanding of the Form of Justice that is independent of what authorities might think it is. It is justice that will help us recognize just acts in this world. These acts are carried out in a just city by a just soul.

In the *Republic*, Plato explains how advanced cities start off as small communities of producers, who craft, farm and build. This is a healthy community, according to Socrates. Unfortunately, human societies need more; they need luxuries. They won't be satisfied with the basics, 'but will have all sorts of furniture like couches and tables, and a wide selection of savouries, perfumes, incense, prostitutes, and pastries'. To obtain such luxuries, more territory is required. This means wars will be fought, so warriors are needed to both invade and protect the city. Some of these warriors will be taught how to rule and become the guardians of the city. The result is a tripartite class structure of producers, warriors and guardians. A city will succeed when there are harmonious interactions between each of these three classes and each knows their place and performs the function best suited to them.

To guarantee stability and this social immobility, during their training the producers, warriors and guardians are told the 'Noble Lie', a story about their origin. This myth explains that:

> *'during the kneading phase, God included gold in the mixture when he was forming those of you who have what it takes to be rulers (which is why the rulers have the greatest privileges), silver when he was forming the auxiliaries, and iron and copper when he was forming the farmers and other workers.'* (the *Republic*)

These metals dictate what each class is capable of and their rightful position and role in society. To prevent warriors becoming tyrannical guardians, they must be given proper education. This education involves instruction on how to better oneself physically (through gymnastics) and mentally (through the arts). Gymnastics involves all physical exercise, not just the agility performances we see at the Olympic Games. Similarly, the arts are not restricted to painting, sculpture and drawing but mainly concern philosophical and scientific pursuits in search of knowledge. The arts will soften the hard nature of the warriors, allowing their intellectual soul to govern their desire to plunder and conquer.

Socrates is quite specific about the requirements: any guardian selected at the age of twenty to be king will also be educated in maths for ten years. Maths is, after all, the elevator up into the World of Forms (see Chapter 3). The guardians are exposed to the dialectic from the ages of thirty to thirty-five. Once they have grasped the dialectic, philosopher kings in training are ready to advise in practical politics until they reach the age of fifty. If shown to be worthy, he may then become the philosopher king after the age of fifty. Philosopher queens are also possible in Plato's republic. If a woman demonstrates the same potential during the rigorous training given to everyone, then she too can be a philosophical ruler. Socrates says: 'Please don't think that what I've been saying doesn't apply equally to any woman in the community with the required natural abilities.' It is, after all, not the body but the soul that makes someone a good philosopher and leader.

The guardians are sectioned off from the rest of society to undergo their training. What this means is that they don't own private property or have families because they must be entirely focused on the state and be willing to make personal sacrifices in order to keep the state in balance. The ideal guardian of the just city is a philosopher like Socrates or Plato who engage in the dialectic, have knowledge of the Forms and the ultimate Form of the Good (which we will discuss in the following section). In knowing the Form of the Good, they know how to make decisions for the good of the city rather than just for themselves.

The soul is a city on a microscopic scale and so also has three parts. A just soul has all its three parts perfectly balanced; it is a well-ordered, virtuous soul that functions effortlessly. Its bronze part has appetites and desires, and practises temperance. The silver part needs courage to function well in order to control the spirited part that expresses emotions. The philosopher rulers have a gold element in their soul that is ruled by the virtue of reason/wisdom. A just soul is a healthy soul that reveals a harmonious interaction between the virtues of wisdom, courage and temperance. Such a soul 'has bound all the factors together and made himself a perfect unity instead of a plurality, self-disciplined and internally attuned'. Socrates is now able to confirm that justice is when 'every individual has to do just one of the jobs relevant to the community, the one for which his nature has best equipped him.'

Justice is to know your place in the world and realize your own potential. This system is a rigidly hierarchical structure and reflects Plato's distrust of democracy. The bronze souls, in being dominated by the appetitive part of their soul, are excused in allowing their desires to take over as they can't do anything else. But the philosopher rulers must make sure their rational soul is in control, otherwise the result will be tyranny (as the examples of Charmides and Critias prove). If all citizens know their place, then there will be a just state. The fact that such a perfect society has never been achieved shows that there is something wrong with this world, and not with the theory, Plato might argue.

For Plato, the prime example of a philosopher king with a just soul – a golden harmonious soul – is Socrates. He is governed by the intellect and knows his place as a philosopher. It is for this reason that he accepts death rather than accepting the deal offered: avoid death but renounce philosophy (in the *Apology*). This is the just thing to do. He is not afraid of death because he knows what awaits him in the afterlife is far greater than what he has experienced in this world of imperfection. He is a just man who has nothing to be ashamed of. He does not hide behind words, as the sophists do, or adornments, as the rich do. Plato portrays him as someone who bears his soul to the world. He cannot do otherwise, and this is what leads him to his death. It is for this reason that Socrates is good for the city. He educates, not corrupts, the youth into perfecting their souls by teaching them how to think dialectically. This is what is good. This is what is just.

Later in his life, Plato seems to have accepted that the ideal state represented in the *Republic* didn't work in this age of Zeus. In the *Laws*, Plato presents an alternative political philosophy that is second best to his ideal of the philosopher king as ruler. He accepts that this world of flux is unprepared for a philosopher ruler. Instead the state should have a statesman at the head who creates and follows laws. These laws will originate from the gods. Citizens will be provided with proper justification (a preamble) for why they should follow these laws. Education will be essential for all citizens and will be considered sacred. The impious will be punished and that includes those who deal:

> 'in prophecy and jugglery of all kinds, and out of their ranks sometimes come tyrants and demagogues and generals and hierophants of private mysteries and the Sophists, as they are termed, with their ingenious devices.'

As you can see, Plato never did make peace with the Sophists.

## The Sun and the Form of the Good

We have seen that a just soul is a virtuous soul ruled by reason. Such a soul has knowledge of the Forms and the Form of the Good. It isn't possible to understand what is just, if we don't understand the Good. Justice is inferior to the Good because the Good is the ultimate Form and the source of all value and goodness in the world. In the *Republic* Socrates explains that

'It's goodness which gives the things we know their truth and makes it possible for people to have knowledge.'

Not knowing that the Good is the only good leads to corruption, according to Plato. The idea that acquiring money is good, suggested by Thrasymachus in the *Republic*, is an illustration of this. Obsessing over money results in people behaving badly, committing crimes and abusing others in order to obtain money. Socrates gives the example of those in authority who crave money; ultimately

> '*if they overtly require money for being in charge, they'll be called hired hands, and if they covertly make money for themselves out of the possession of power, they'll be called thieves.*'

For money to become good (participate in the Good), it must be used well and for this, we have to have knowledge of how to use it. Knowledge of the Good can provide us with this knowledge by telling us whether something is good or bad. Consequently, a good life is a life lived according to what is good because we know the Good. Good is the ultimate object of the philosophical quest and, according to Plato, it is what all human beings desire deep down. Nobody is satisfied with what appears to be good, 'It's the reality of goodness they want; no one thinks at all highly of mere appearance in this sphere.'

Unfortunately, we never find out what the Good is from Plato. This is something we should be able to find out for ourselves now we have been equipped with the skills of the dialectic. Plato does describe 'a child' of the Good in the simile of the sun:

> *'The sun is the child of goodness [...] as goodness stands*
> *in the intelligible realm to intelligence and the things we*
> *know, so in the visible realm the sun stands to sight and*
> *the things we see.'* (the *Republic*)

The sun provides light that allows for the viewing of objects. The Form of the Good provides light in the sense that it offers the truth about the Forms. So, the Good shines light on the truth in the same way as the sun shines light on objects. The Good is the cause of knowledge and truth and makes both possible. But, warns Socrates, we mustn't 'identify either of them with goodness, which should be rated even more highly.'

The sun has a further role to play; it is responsible for existence in the visible world. Without the sun, there wouldn't be life. In the same way, the Good is the ultimate principle of 'being' and, consequently, the entire world is good because the Form of the Good is the cause of it.

## Pleasure and the Good Life

Some of Socrates' interlocuters consider actions that give people pleasure to be good, and those that cause pain to be bad. Plato points out that it is not as straightforward as this, and explains why in both the *Republic* and *Philebus*. In the *Republic*, Socrates explains that pleasure can take different forms and what is pleasure for one can be pain for another. Pleasure can come in the form of appetite (physical pleasures), which are characteristic of bronze souls. Whereas for silver souls, pleasure can be honour. However, the pleasures of golden souls, of wisdom and learning the truth – the pleasures of the philosopher – are real pleasures in comparison to the artificial pleasures of appetite or honour. Plato is not suggesting that philosophers can't have any other pleasures; they can. But philosophers know which pleasures are good because they are aware of all three (appetite, honour and wisdom) and in an ideal position to judge that only wisdom is real.

In *Philebus*, Plato addresses other pleasures that can contribute to a good life. He calls these pure pleasures and they are:

> *'Those which have to do with the colours we call beautiful, with figures, with most scents, with musical sounds: in short, with anything which, since it involves imperceptible, painless lack, provides perceptible, pleasant replenishment which is uncontaminated by pain.'*

Acquiring wisdom fits this description perfectly. There are, however, some impure pleasures that accompany virtue that are valuable in a good life. The impure pleasures of eating or drinking when accompanied with the virtue of moderation, for example. But impure pleasures are derived from pain or discomfort, Plato tells us, unlike pure pleasures. Socrates gives the example of the impure pleasure of quenching thirst where 'thirst is disruption and pain, but when liquid replenishes what was formerly parched, that is pleasure.'

Furthermore, all impure pleasures are false pleasures in that they involve dishonesty, self-deception and do not correspond to facts. We are dishonest with ourselves if we believe that impure pleasures will last and are not the result of something we will lack again. The pleasure of fantasising about winning 'an incredible amount of money' is a false pleasure, for example. This too is derived from a lack: a lack of having enough money. Only pure pleasures are true pleasures. But Plato is aware that a life without impure pleasures is not a human life. Ultimately, Plato thinks we should aim to feel neither pleasure nor pain: like true philosophers are able to do. We should be concerned with what lies beyond the senses and beyond this mundane world that produces pleasure and pain so as to be closer to the gods.

## Piety and the Gods

Socrates does not, as his accusers claim in the *Apology*, worship new spiritual beings. Both Socrates and Plato were pious men; they believed in the gods, whether they liked them or not, and took part in religious festivals and rites. A religious occasion was often the reason for Socrates' venture out into Athens town, giving his interlocuters the opportunity to detain him. In the *Republic*, for example, he is on his way home from worshipping the goddess Bendis when Cephalus and Polemarchus invite him to their house.

The Athenians in Plato's time were polytheistic (believing in many gods). They worshipped the Olympian gods (Zeus and his family) and other gods from their own culture as well as imported gods from neighbouring cultures. Bendis, mentioned in the *Republic*, for example, was from the Balkan region and had similarities with the Olympian goddess Artemis (goddess of hunting, chastity and childbirth). Asclepius, mentioned in Socrates' dying words in *Phaedo*, was the imported god of medicine from Epidaurus. Socrates asks Crito to offer the sacrifice of a cock to Asclepius as his last request.

Do the gods give us morality or is it based on philosophical reasoning? This is the question laid out in *Euthyphro*. Euthyphro is a priest who is about to put his own father on trial for allowing one of his workers to die in a ditch. The worker killed another, and so Euthyphro's father threw him in a ditch while he worked out what to do with him. In the meantime, the labourer died. Socrates questions Euthyphro's piety by asking him how he knows what his father did was wrong. If he knows what he is doing is pious (what the gods want), he must know what piety is. Euthyphro's answer is that 'what all the gods love is pious and holy, and the opposite which they all hate, impious.'

The problem is that if the gods love what is pious because it is pious, then piety is not something that comes from the gods, it is something they love. If this is the case, then it must come from elsewhere, Socrates points out. By the end of the dialogue, no satisfactory definition of piety is found but this doesn't hinder Euthyphro from continuing to indict his father for murder.

The same principles apply to justice. This too can't be defined by appealing to the gods. The gods are not responsible for justice, they just love it. Plato would regard the dialectic as just (it leads us to the Forms of Piety, Justice and Goodness). As the gods love piety and justice and, therefore, the dialectic, the gods must be inferior to this, unless the dialectic is derived from the gods. But Plato leaves us in the dark about this. Maybe the gods use the dialectic to be informed by the Good? Whatever the case, Plato places the Good in the highest regard, above the gods who are informed by the Good but are not the Good themselves. The reason for this is that the perfect, eternal Form of the Good is more secure than the arbitrary whims of the gods. This is perfectly consistent with Plato's ethical system and with those forms of monotheism, indebted to Plato's thought, that recognize no real distinction between the eternal and unchanging nature of God (Good) and the will of God and so no possibility of divine whim contradicting the Good.

In the 'Reign of Cronos' myth from the *Statesman*, Plato refers to an age when everything was opposite – harmonious and utopian – which, for Plato, was the right way. In a depiction that resembles that of the Garden of Eden from Genesis in the Bible, Socrates explains that under Cronos (head of the Titans):

> *'...there were no forms of government, or separate possession of women and children; for all men rose again from the earth, having no memory of the past. And although they had nothing of this sort, the earth gave them fruits in abundance, which grew on trees and shrubs unbidden, and were not planted by the hand of man. And they dwelt naked, and mostly in the open air, for the temperature of their seasons was mild; and they had no beds, but lay on soft couches of grass, which grew plentifully out of the earth. Such was the life of man in the days of Cronos.'*

That age came to an end when 'the pilot of the universe let the helm go' (we assume the pilot is Cronos). Then 'Fate and innate desire' caused the world to rotate in the opposite direction, causing earthquakes that destroyed many animals. The Age of Zeus and the Olympians dawned, and everything became imperfect and wrong. The new gods tried to help humanity: Prometheus gave the gift of fire, Hephaestus gave the arts, and Athene gave seeds. Humans were left to fend for themselves in an everchanging world that they had initiated but were also slave to. With certain differences, the myth resembles the Fall of Man as taught in Christianity.

Philosopher kings may have been able to rule in the age of Cronos, but not in this new age of change and uncertainty governed by inferior gods who are prone to spiteful and destructive behaviour. Plato's ideal god (a god like Cronos maybe) is purely good and only creates good things. In *Timaeus*, Plato describes how a craftsman-like god made the best possible universe we now occupy. It is good because it is ordered mathematically and the god, in making it, is virtuous in using reason. This is a god worthy of piety, although not over and above the Good.

# Conclusion

Plato introduced us to the dialectic as the method of obtaining certainty, knowledge and a good life. By means of the dialectic, he tells us that there are many things that lie beyond the physical world of matter. He has helped us find out what we can know, while at the same time questioning those ordinary things we claim to know. He has given us hope – where the natural philosophers and sophists failed – by divulging that there are things we can be certain of and that we can know. Plato has explained why the tendency to rely on the empirical is unjustifiable: it can't provide certainty. Science can't give us the full story, but philosophy can help to place science in the bigger picture. This bigger picture includes that which is reliable; what is eternal and unchangeable, of which the empirical is only a reflection. Plato offered us the Forms as candidates for the eternal and unchangeable, but we don't have to accept them. He would have welcomed other suggestions as long as they are supported by reasoning using the dialectic. The dialectic is the absolute certainty and should be conducted fully and sincerely.

The dialectic exposes the inconsistences in our day-to-day language and how we shouldn't just take things for granted. Knowing yourself is the most fundamental of these assumptions for Plato and it seems that there are very few who have this knowledge. Nobody knows who they really are, what they consist of, and what makes them act the way they do. Nobody has stood still to consider whether they know anything and how they might know this. In highlighting this, Plato has awoken his self, our self, the self. He has also warned us of the dire consequences that can follow from listening to those who are ignorant of their self. This lesson in humility and caution is one we could all heed.

Plato's philosophy might be looked at as foundational. It has been used to justify certain religious beliefs, most commonly by replacing the rational Forms with the divine mind. Plato also taught the West that it shouldn't just live a life that is ruled by the physical. Although his way of thinking is something associated with religion because religion relies on the existence and superiority of the non-physical, it doesn't have to be just for the religious. As true today as it obviously was then, a life focusing on physical pleasures – as Plato pointed out centuries ago – will only lead to unhappiness, either for yourself or for others or both. This is something that the Western world has forgotten as it becomes increasingly reliant on science and physicalism (the belief that only matter exists). Alongside this philosophical physicalism, there has been a wider social tendency towards economic materialism and consumerism which ignores the qualitative, non-physical, mental aspects of life (something that Marxist materialism critiques). Physical pleasures are short-lived, whereas pleasures of the mind (what nineteenth-century philosopher John Stuart Mill called higher pleasures) are more lasting. Reading a philosophy book, Plato would insist, is going to have a more lasting effect on your happiness than going shopping and spending lots of money. A person is not just their body, Plato teaches us.

On a more positive note, the basic principles underpinning the dialectic might work in favour of science today. When politicians tell us they are 'following the science' (this might be in relation to Covid-19, or the environment, or anything else), are they following '*the* science', or just what *some* scientists are saying from within *particular* scientific disciplines? We have learned from Plato that it must be the latter. Despite this, we could foster a more realistic and forgiving attitude towards the provisional and fallible but still essential input of science to public policy.

The dialogues may seem frustrating at times when conclusions aren't reached, but perhaps this is something we should learn to appreciate instead of wanting quick and easy answers. This is the key to a good and virtuous life, after all. Being virtuous involves sacrificing bodily temptations and superficial responses to fundamental questions (like those proposed by sophists or politicians). Only a selected few – the gold souls – are capable of this, according to Plato, but maybe he underestimated the amount of gold souls that exist. Who is to say that there isn't a gold soul potential in everyone? We need more philosophers to love everyone – in a Platonic way – and teach us the dialectical method so that we may perfect ourselves and each other.

An unexamined life is not worth living, Socrates said in his *Apology*. The aim of this book is to explain why this is the case by introducing you to Plato's metaphysics, epistemology and ethics through his many works. Examining what it is that exists and how we can know this, is inextricably linked to how we should act. This is the underlying message in all of Plato's works and this is what life is all about. Every Platonic dialogue is also a lesson in the dialectical method of philosophy. Reading one of his dialogues is a practice in virtue and is a lesson on how to become virtuous. This should be all the encouragement you need to examine Plato's work further and to start implementing the dialectic when you are dealing with knowledge and what you think exists.

One final word on Socrates and his importance for Plato. Socrates may or may not have uttered the words, phrases and ideas as they appear in Plato's works, but it was Plato's interpretation of them that has reached us. Plato is the one who tells us what it is we can know, who teaches us the dialectic and how to be virtuous. Socrates is a useful way of presenting an exemplar of a philosopher king who loves his interlocuters in the only way he knows how to: by teaching them the dialectic. He is the true lover of wisdom. But maybe he is not the only one, does Plato not deserve this title as well?

> **Socrates:** *Plato, do you agree that our discussions about humankind and the search for knowledge are more than a mere daydream?*
>
> **Plato:** *My dearest Socrates, as genuine philosophers we know that this is just the beginning.*
>
> **Socrates:** *How do you propose we continue then?*
>
> **Plato:** *We must proceed from the basic assumption.*
>
> **Socrates:** *What then might this assumption be?*
>
> **Plato:** *Why, the most solid of daydreams! That indeed we know nothing.*

# Appendix: List of Characters

The following is a list of names and characters referred to in this book and, in brackets, in which of Plato's texts they appear.

**Adeimantus:** Plato's brother (the *Republic* and *Parmenides*)

**Agathon:** a poet who wrote tragedies (the *Symposium*)

**Alcibiades:** an Athenian statesman (*Alcibiades*, the *Symposium* and *Protagoras*)

**Antiphon:** Plato's half-brother (*Parmenides*)

**Anytus:** a craftsman and one of the accusers of Socrates (the *Apology*)

**Aristocles:** Plato's real name

**Aristophanes:** a comic poet who ridiculed Socrates in his plays (the *Symposium*)

**Charmides:** Plato's uncle, a sophist who became one of the 'Thirty Tyrants' (*Charmides*)

**Clitophon:** an Athenian oligarch and friend of Thrasymachus (*Clitophon*)

**Cratylus:** a Heraclitan philosopher from Athens (*Cratylus*)

**Critias:** Plato's mother's cousin, a sophist who became one of the 'Thirty Tyrants' (*Charmides, Protagoras, Timaeus* and *Critias*)

**Crito:** a friend of Socrates (*Crito, Euthydemus* and *Phaedo*)

**Euthyphro:** a priest and soothsayer who takes his father to trial (*Euthyphro*)

**Glaucon:** Plato's older brother (the *Republic* and *Parmenides*)

**Gorgias:** a famous sophist, who earns some respect from Socrates (*Gorgias*)

**Hippias:** a sophist (the *Apology, Hippias Major, Hippias Minor* and *Protagoras*)

**Hippothales:** a youth who has erotic feelings for Lysis (*Lysis*)

**Ion:** a performer of poetry (*Ion*)

**Laches:** an Athenian general (*Laches*)

**Lycon:** an orator and one of the accusers of Socrates (the *Apology*)

**Lysis:** a youth who is the focus of Hippothales' erotic feelings (*Lysis*)

**Meletus:** a poet and one of the accusers of Socrates (the *Apology*)

**Menexenus:** a friend of Lysis (*Lysis* and *Menexenus*)

**Meno:** a sophist, student of Gorgias and ambitious military leader (*Meno*)

**Parmenides:** a famous pre-Socratic philosopher who argued that all reality is one (*Parmenides*)

**Phaedo:** a follower of Socrates and a Pythagorean (*Phaedo*)

**Phaedrus:** a rhetorician (*Phaedrus* and the *Symposium*)

**Philebus:** a hedonist, promoting the pursuit of pleasure, and probably a fictional character (*Philebus*)

**Protagoras:** a famous sophist full of his own self-importance (*Protagoras*)

**Protarchus:** a hedonist, promoting the pursuit of pleasure, learnt his arguments from the sophists (*Philebus*)

**Speusippus:** Plato's nephew and successor to the Academy

**Socrates:** Plato's teacher and the protagonist in his dialogues (*Alcibiades*, the *Apology*, *Charmides*, *Clitophon*, *Critias*, *Crito*, *Cratylus*, *Euthydemus*, *Euthyphro*, *Gorgias*, *Hippias* (both minor and major), *Ion*, *Laches*, *Lysis*, *Menexenus*, *Meno*, *Parmenides*, *Phaedo*, *Phaedrus*, *Philebus*, *Protagoras*, the *Republic*, the *Sophist*, the *Statesman* (as the young Socrates) the *Symposium*, *Theaetetus* and *Timaeus*)

**Theaetetus:** a mathematician and student of Theodorus (*Theaetetus* and the *Sophist*)

**Theodorus:** a mathematician (*Theaetetus*, the *Sophist* and the *Statesman*)

**Thrasymachus:** a sophist (the *Republic*)

**Timaeus:** a fictional character in Plato's dialogues (*Timaeus* and *Critias*)

**Zeno:** a student of Parmenides (*Parmenides*)

# Bibliography

## Works by Plato

Plato, *Early Socratic Dialogues*, trans. by Trevor J. Saunders, Iain Lane, Donald Watt and Robin Waterfield (2005) London, New York, Toronto: Penguin Books.

Plato, *Gorgias*, trans. by Walter Hamilton (1971) London, New York, Toronto: Penguin Books.

Plato, *Parmenides*, trans. by Benjamin Jowett (2011) Seaside, OR: Watchmaking Publishing.

Plato, *Philebus*, trans. by Robin Waterfield (2006) London, New York, Victoria: Penguin Books.

Plato, *Protagoras and Meno*, trans. by W. K. C. Guthrie (1956) London, New York, Toronto: Penguin Books.

Plato, *Republic*, trans. by Robin Waterfield (1993) Oxford, New York, Toronto: Oxford University Press.

Plato, *Sophist and Statesman*, trans. by Benjamin Jowett (2018) Mineola, New York: Dover Publications.

Plato, *Symposium and Phaedrus*, trans. by Benjamin Jowett (1993) Mineola, New York: Dover Publications.

Plato, *Theaetetus*, trans. by Robin Waterfield (2004) London, New York, Victoria: Penguin Books.

**Plato,** *The Laws*, trans. by Trevor J. Saunders (2005) London, New York, Victoria: Penguin Books.

**Plato,** *The Trial and Death of Socrates*, trans. by Benjamin Jowett (1992) Mineola, New York: Dover Publications.

**Plato,** *Timaeus and Critias*, trans. by Desmond Lee (1977) London, New York, Victoria: Penguin Books.

## Other works cited

**Adamson,** Peter (2014) *Classical Philosophy: A history of philosophy without any gaps, Volume I*. Oxford, New York, Toronto: Oxford University Press.

**Adamson,** Peter (2018) *Philosophy in the Hellenistic & Roman Worlds: A history of philosophy without any gaps, Volume II*. Oxford, New York, Toronto: Oxford University Press.

**Annas,** Julia (2003) *Ancient Philosophy, A Very Short Introduction*. Oxford, New York, Toronto: Oxford University Press.

**Annas,** Julia (2003) *Plato, A Very Short Introduction*. Oxford, New York, Toronto: Oxford University Press.

**Copleston,** Frederick (1946) *A History of Philosophy, Vol. I: Greece and Rome*. London and NY: Continuum. (This edition 2012)

**Ferguson,** John (1970) *Socrates, A source book compiled by John Ferguson*. London and Basingstoke: MacMillan for the Open University Press.

**Gottlieb,** Anthony (2001) *The Dream of Reason, A History of Philosophy from the Greeks to the Renaissance*. London, New York, Toronto: Penguin Books.

**Gregory,** John (1999) *The Neoplatonists, A Reader*. London and New York: Routledge.

**Hanegraaff,** Wouter J. (2012) *Esotericism and the Academy*. Cambridge, New York, Melbourne: Cambridge University Press.

**Heinaman,** Robert (2003) 'Plato: Metaphysics and Epistemology' in C.W.W. Taylor (ed.), *From the Beginning to Plato: Routledge History of Philosophy, Vol. I*. London and New York: Routledge.

**Kahn,** Charles H. (2015) *Plato and the Post-Socratic Dialogue.* Cambridge, New York, Melbourne: Cambridge University Press.

**Kraut,** Richard (ed.) (1995) *The Cambridge Companion to Plato.* Cambridge, New York, Melbourne: Cambridge University Press.

**Pappas,** Nickolas (1995) *Plato and the Republic.* London: Routledge.

**Whitehead,** A. N. (1929) *Process and Reality.* New Jersey: Prentice Hall. (This edition 1979)

## Biography

Dr Karen Parham is Lecturer in Philosophy for Warwickshire College Group. She has a PhD in Philosophy and Dutch Studies, Master of Arts degrees in European Philosophy and Art & Cultural Sciences, PGCE in Philosophy and Bachelor of Arts degrees in Dutch Studies and Philosophy. She is an independent scholar and freelance writer of academic articles and books, creative non-fiction and fiction for young adults and children.

## Acknowledgements

Many thanks to Alice and Sarah for helping to bring this book about. I am also indebted to my partner, James McGhee, my father, Stephen Parham, and Jonathan Birch, the series editor and academic adviser for taking the time to read through this work and making helpful suggestions.

## Picture Credits

**Fig. 1** 'Bust of Plato'. Jean Housen (https://commons.wikimedia.org/wiki/File:20140416_corfu232-cropped-bg.jpg), https://creativecommons.org/licenses/by-sa/4.0/legalcode. **Fig. 2** 'Bust of Socrates'. Sting (https://commons.wikimedia.org/wiki/File:Socrates_Louvre.jpg), „Socrates Louvre", https://creativecommons.org/licenses/by-sa/2.5/legalcode. **Fig. 3**. *'The Death of Socrates* painted by Jacques-Louis David in 1787. Jacques-Louis David artist QS:P170,Q83155 (https://commons.wikimedia.org/wiki/File:David_-_The_Death_of_Socrates.jpg), „David - The Death of Socrates", marked as public domain, more details on Wikimedia Commons: https://commons.wikimedia.org/wiki/Template:PD-old. **Fig. 4** 'Fragment of Plato's *Republic*'. Platon (https://commons.wikimedia.org/wiki/File:P._Oxy._LII_3679.jpg), „P. Oxy. LII 3679", marked as public domain, more details on Wikimedia Commons: https://commons.wikimedia.org/wiki/Template:PD-old. **Fig. 5** *'The School of Athens* painted by Raphael between 1509–1511. All the philosophers depicted sought knowledge of first causes. Plato and Aristotle appear as the central figures, with Socrates in brown robes, ninth from left.' Raphael artist QS:P170,Q5597 (https://commons.wikimedia.org/wiki/File:"The_School_of_Athens"_by_Raffaello_Sanzio_da_Urbino.jpg), „"The School of Athens" by Raffaello Sanzio da Urbino", marked as public domain, more details on Wikimedia Commons: https://commons.wikimedia.org/wiki/Template:PD-old. **Fig. 6** 'An illustration of The Allegory of the Cave from Plato's *Republic*'. 4edges (https://commons.wikimedia.org/wiki/File:An_Illustration_of_The_Allegory_of_the_Cave,_from_Plato's_Republic.jpg), https://creativecommons.org/licenses/by-sa/4.0/legalcode.

# Who the hell is

This exciting new series of books sets out to explore the life and theories of the world's leading intellectuals in a clear and understandable way. The series currently includes the following subject areas:

## Art History | Psychology | Philosophy | Sociology | Politics

### Available now:

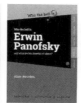

For more information about forthcoming titles in the Who the hell is...? series, go to: **www.whothehellis.co.uk**.

If any of our readers would like to put in a request for a particular intellectual to be included in our series, then please contact us at **info@whothehellis.co.uk**.

Printed in Great Britain
by Amazon

61791307R00066